THE NATIVE LITERACY SOURCE OF MEDICINE

TAKING CARE OF THE CARE GIVERS

Nisheducator

authorHOUSE®

AuthorHouse™
1663 Liberty Drive
Bloomington, IN 47403
www.authorhouse.com
Phone: 1-800-839-8640

First published by AuthorHouse 9/29/2009

ISBN: 978-1-4490-2089-7 (sc)

Library of Congress Control Number: 2009909875

Printed in the United States of America
Bloomington, Indiana

This book is printed on acid-free paper.

Taking care of the caregivers is something I came to understand after leaving formal teaching in the classroom to work with literacy learners. So many of the people in a caregiver capacity in the Aboriginal community struggle to make a difference with the training they have acquired in mainstream programs and courses. Four important elements that create barriers for the helper and the individual in need of help: 1. There is a profound lack of understanding of the root cause on the part of both sides. 2. Euro western training treats the symptoms not the cause. 3. Funding with its accountability requirements invariably comes from outside sources creating limitations. 4. Inter-generational impact of residential school and colonialism.

I have also come to understand that the reason there appears to be no progress is again the euro western-based theory of intervention rather than prevention. Systemic opposition to prevention is entrenched in policies in education, social work, and justice. As my mother would say, "laws are created to enforce laws" resulting in no social justice.

If Aboriginal people were programmed to hear truth and reconciliation through their own people out of their own ideology, social justice would make a comeback not just for them but the "others" as well. A further dilemma is *accredited* individuals, who fear a loss of money and resist the promotion of such a fail proof undertaking. Combating this impasse is the inspiration behind this book. This book was originally written as…a thesis submitted in conformity with the requirements for the degree of Master of Arts at the Department of Sociology and Equity Studies in Education, Ontario Institute for Studies in Education of the University of Toronto under the original title of Binary Opposition between Aboriginal and Non-Aboriginal Holistic Method Impedes Success in Native Literacy. There's been lot of "water under the bridge" since it was originally written but I have left it intact for the most part.

I am a woman
an Indian woman.
I am sister, daughter, grandchild,
Wife, mother, auntie, grandmother
I love, teach, protect and share.
One day for you that will be enough,
And you will know,
What all my relations already know.
We are equal and you are my relation too.
Karen B. McClain
OTC, B.A., M.A.

Abstract

Wholistic, Aboriginal socialization is presented as the foundation of literacy for the Aboriginal population. A definition representing the worldview and reality of Aboriginal society is offered to specifically meet the literacy needs of the Aboriginal community. Intergenerational trauma presented as the origin of several levels of underlying needs in the Aboriginal community clarifies the call for literacy training that will guide the individual to read their history and "read situations, social structures and social locations" to enable better access to mainstream institutions and to build success and identity.

Literacy is discussed in the context of the Ministry of Training, Colleges and University program, under which Native literacy practitioners have disclosed policy that does not represent Aboriginal stakeholders.

Content is based on an extensive literature review, life experience, university studies and reflective teaching in the Aboriginal community over a 40-year period.

Acknowledgements

During my preparation for writing the thesis this book is based on I struggled to stay in the present. I had a very hard time pulling back from the vision of what the future would bring when Native Literacy and Education are in fact based in Native worldview for I had witnessed it more than once in reality in a classroom. The understandings and awareness that I brought to the paper had been offered to me over a sixty-year period by my grandparents, parents, aunts and uncles, siblings, students, teachers and colleagues.

The understandings that I now bring to this book four years later are based on the feedback and understandings gained through working with Native literacy practitioners and a recent action research project in the field of Native literacy.

I have been told by my elders "you will see your beliefs and attitudes in your children and grandchildren". My daughters and grandchildren have contributed not only patience and support but also wisdom and intuition to persist. Miigwech!

Forty years of teaching in the Aboriginal education field have challenged me to ride the ebb and flow of policy, government agenda, knowledge creation and curriculum development. I acknowledge my first principal, Sister Perpetua deceased, who set me on the road of challenging the status quo in Aboriginal education. I thank Lori Jacobs, former education manager of Curve Lake First Nation for allowing me to pilot my version of Aboriginal education and which now provides me with confirmation that Aboriginal world view in a learning environment facilitates resounding success.

Thanks and recognition go to the literacy workers who accepted me into their midst and allowed me to share for the last seven years what I have learned on my journey through the institutions of education. Thanks to Pat Powell, executive director of the Peterborough Native Literacy Program. She set me on this portion of my life journey, and allowed me to bounce ideas and yet keep me mindful me of policy and limitations.

Chi-Miigwech, to Dr. Judy Iseke-Barnes and Dr. Eileen Antone whose guidance and trust made it possible for me to continue my challenge to the status quo of the Aboriginal community.

TABLE OF CONTENTS

Abstract vii

Acknowledgements viii

Chapter 1 — Introduction 1
Background to The Problem 1
Presentation of the ProblemVignettes of Students
"Caught in the System" 4
Assumptions 6
Contribution of This Thesis to the Field of Native Literacy 7
Defining Terms 8
Research Questions 9
My Connection to These Questions 10
Structure of the Thesis 12

**Chapter 2 — Ontario Literacy: Literacy for Liberation or
Literacy for Conformity?** 15
History and Development of Ontario Literacy 17
Whatever happened to "community" in
Community Programs? 24
Literacy Funding: Accountability V.S. The Learner 27
Objectives of Literacy and Basic Skills Programs 31
    Lifelong Learning 31
    Quality Service 32
    Learner Centered For Learners Most in Need 32
    Accountability: Political 34
    Accountability: Learner and Community 36
    Literacy Training and Employment 36
Conclusion 37

Chapter 3 — Ontario Native Literacy: A Colonial Reality 41
Literacy and Basic Skills Program (LBS) Applied
to Native literacy 42

Life-long learning...42
Quality Service 43
Learner Centered for Learners Most in Need..................44
Accountability: Political...45
Accountability: Learner and Community......................46
Literacy Training and Employment..............................48
Recognizing the Need to Decolonize 50
Native Literacy Must be Unique 51
Conclusion 55

Chapter 4 — Wholistic Native Literacy 59
Introduction..59
Native Wholistic Literacy and Pedagogy 64
Healing in the Medicine Wheel Approach 66
Healing in Relevant Curriculum 68
Post Colonialism a Misleading Notion That Creates Barriers 71
Illiteracy: A Lack of Effective Education/
Socialization/Literacy...73
Native Literacy Revolutionized 75
Four Origins of Needs...76
Content: The Compelling Tool..82
Conclusion 83

Chapter 5 — Summary and Conclusions.............................. 85
Summary 85
Conclusions 88

References **97**

CHAPTER 1

INTRODUCTION

BACKGROUND TO THE PROBLEM

Implementing an Aboriginal concept of wholistic literacy would change the helpfulness of Native literacy. Genuine "Native" literacy cannot happen without articulating an Aboriginal concept of wholistic literacy and applying it to literacy training.

A persistent need to assemble the Aboriginal concept of wholistic into literacy training has become even more pronounced in 2005. Current trends of the Ministry of Training, Colleges, and Universities towards using on-line learning and literacy training exclusively for employment training not only belies the understood connotation of literacy but it also denies the reality that Aboriginal communities live with unprecedented poverty based in unemployment and lack of employment opportunities available to Aboriginal people.

The term "literacy" generally raises thoughts of "learning to read". In fact, wholistic literacy training is much more than that. It means "reading the word and the world" according to Paulo Friere and Donald Macedo (1987). Discussion of the meaning of literacy has been documented since the 1930s indicating that early in the recognition of illiteracy, a wholistic approach was contemplated. Articles and literature indicate that the learner was indeed considered as a part of a whole (Roeher Institute 1999, Newman 1994).

If 'social integration means strengthening a diverse country's capacity for sustainable development, it must equalize all groups enjoyment of freedom and resources, without sacrificing their underlying diversity in the process." (Barsh 1994:37) In his discussion of population growth, isolation, standard of living and inaccurate, statistical representation of the Aboriginal population in

1

Canada Russel Barsh, graduate of Harvard Law School and current Director of the Samish Indian Nation research program lends much to this discussion of the need to re present Native literacy. The "Aboriginal baby boom generation" aging into the labour force explains the increasingly high unemployment situation in Aboriginal communities. The extreme poverty, and unemployment in the Aboriginal community, urban and reserve, is sufficiently documented in journals, documentaries, and statistics (Statistics Canada 2001, Indian and Northern Affairs 2003, Minister of Supply and Services 1996, Chapman, McCaskill and Newhouse 1991, Barsh 1994, Haddad and Spivey 1992, Lamontagne 2004).

When literacy was put under the umbrella of the Ministry of Training, Colleges and Universities in Ontario the intent of literacy became employment at all costs as opposed to facilitating learners in their endeavor to change their quality of living. Dictates of the "Workforce Workplace Literacy Initiative" would have learners streamlined into low-paying jobs that barely cover expenses that in fact provide less than current Ontario Works (Social Assistance) when transportation and childcare costs are factored into the picture. In effect, literacy training has become one of the tools that maintain the power and economic status quo (Mullaly 1997:138-159).

There is little progress in meeting Native literacy issues. In 1982 Jackson, McCaskill and Hall wrote, "agendas of government funding agencies interests in preserving the status quo run counter to the interests of Native movements in developing skills and knowledge to bring about changes in the forces causing their exploitation and oppression" (Jackson et al 1982). They go on to say that "initiatives in Native training and research have been stifled, undermined, defused, delayed or simply eliminated by forces hostile to Native self-determination". Recent 2005 activities with the Ontario Native Literacy Coalition, Workforce/Workplace Literacy and Ministry of Training, Colleges and Universities (MTCU) distinctly place this 1982 statement in the present. Despite a year of refuting and attempting to address the negative impact workforce/workplace literacy could have in the Aboriginal community, MTCU through Quill, the provincial network awarded the contract of Train Ontario, have pursued a forceful agenda which ignores the inappropriateness of employment goals in Aboriginal communities – inappropriate not only in terms of lack of employment opportunities but also the documented need to heal impacts of colonization first.

People always live up to our expectations no matter what they are. In other words stereotyping can and will create a self-fulfilling prophecy. A web search for a definition of self-fulfilling prophecy produced; a "concept developed by Robert K. Merton to explain how a belief or expectation, whether correct or not, affects the outcome of a situation or the way a person (or group) will behave." In psychology I studied it as "conditioning". Rosenthal and Jacobson (1992) describe it as "the process by which a person's expectations about someone can lead to that person behaving in ways which confirm the expectations".

Since becoming a literacy instructor in 2000 after twenty-four years of teaching at the primary level in the elementary system in Aboriginal reserve settings, the significance of this statement and its long term effects has gelled into an appalling epitaph of Aboriginal education. Aboriginal people have generally adopted and enforced this self-fulfilling prophecy of inferiority and dependency, the "culture of poverty" taught to them through Native education that Mullaly speaks to (Mullaly 1997:122-23). Aboriginal peoples have mastered all that has been taught them. Read the historian's account of Canadian history. Aboriginal peoples have been labeled not only "learning disabled" but also "developmentally challenged" to use current vernacular. Since early contact with the allegedly "superior race" this labeling has generated a false consciousness of dependency and inferiority. Evidence of what Aboriginal people have been taught is glaring. Historically Canadian Native education on reserves has been substandard (Battiste in Battiste and Barman 1995: vii-xx, Chrisjohn, Young and Mauran 1997:68). Academic knowledge is the organizing principle of all education and this is translated into reserve schools through the Ontario provincial curriculum. Lacking in wholistic thought it doesn't address interconnectedness, self-awareness, identity, self-worth and skills to operate in the mainstream with its imposed limitations. Academic knowledge is the premier focus of the Ontario provincial curriculum. However, the intent of Native education has never been to reach provincial standards, the arena all Aboriginal young people must eventually enter. They must leave the reserve setting or enter distance education.

When Aboriginal people reach back to pre-contact history there is an enduring core curriculum to lead them out of the third world misery (as described in Mercredi 1994:45, Dei, Hall and Rosenberg 2000:9, Minister of Supply and Services 1996:59). That core curriculum can be found in the teachings of the medicine wheel. "The medicine wheel can be used as a model of what human beings could become of they decided and acted to develop their full potential." (Bopp, Bopp, Brown and Lee 1985:35) There is a clear requirement of spiritual, emotional, physical and intellectual growth. Also, within the medicine wheel is the teaching of interconnectedness – a code that binds individuals and communities to the care and nurturing of one another and the earth.

Looking at the reality of Aboriginal communities indicates a colossal need for change, perhaps a return to the original values that made for sound, spiritual communities. Researching and experiencing the offerings of literacy indicates to me that change will not happen through literacy, the last resort for individuals who have been failed by Canadian institutions.

PRESENTATION OF THE PROBLEM
VIGNETTES OF STUDENTS "CAUGHT IN THE SYSTEM"

Individuals, who have mustered the courage to approach a literacy program despite the stereotyped, disdain literacy wears, are to be honoured for their tenacity. Literacy carries a stigma and an aura of poverty and irresponsibility (Veeman 2002) that individuals choose not to attach them selves to. "The myth of the illiterate savage that predominated in European thought" (Barman, Hebert, McCaskill 1987: 29) lingers on.

I will present vignettes of composites of students who may benefit from wholistic literacy. All descriptions are composites of clients and the names are fictional.

Sam a forty-seven year old Aboriginal grandmother; Janet a twenty-six year old single, Aboriginal new mom, Mark an Aboriginal young man just recently off the street and John an Aboriginal university drop out, all have a grade twelve diploma (OSSD). In addition, they are all on assistance from Ontario Works (OW), live on the periphery of society, live in poverty and live under complete and utter control of the state. But most revealing of all, they all suffer issues with illiteracy. They are in good company. My experience informs me that many young professional Aboriginal people, despite their college and university certificates and degrees do not have sufficient general (living) knowledge to thrive in their chosen career in their preferred environment exposing a further form of literacy need for Aboriginal people who have been socialized in isolated, Aboriginal communities.

Sam cannot read or spell. Violence forced her to move to the city and develop unique ways to parent and survive. Sam speaks her Ojibway language, knows medicines and the stories of her family and community history, but she has grown up believing that she is dyslexic because of huge gaps in her learning. Gaps created by having to parent her siblings from the age of seven. As a result of her growth in Native literacy Sam wrote a book about surviving in the city. Sam's "teacher" who accompanied Sam from typing illegible grocery lists, to writing her story, used Aboriginal history and word searches drawn from teachings of the Anishnabe way to motivate Sam to read and spell. Sam has a better understanding of the behaviour and attitudes in her community and it has calmed her bitterness at what she perceives as lack of support. Some day her son might look her up and bring her grandchildren to visit. Sam looks forward to sharing what she has learned.

Janet desperately wants to learn how to read the books she has collected for her new baby. Several years of dysfunction has awakened her to the reality of illiteracy and she wants something better for her child. Janet accepts that it will probably take a very long time because not only has she been convinced by the education system that she is dyslexic but she also meets with daily resistance from her spouse and Ontario Works (OW). She is determined and hopeful now that she too has found a teacher with time for one-to-one tutoring, who astonishingly enough created exercises specifically for her needs. Janet hopes to write her General Education Development test – Grade Twelve Equivalency (GED). Weeks from now when she finds the money to repay her teacher for the GED book Janet is hoping to return to her studies. Janet promised her tutor that she

would not be like "those others" who got the money for the book and didn't return to pay or to their studies because they didn't pay. A bigger need for the book money came up. The baby is better now and doesn't require so many diapers a day.

Mark has found an educator ten years after being "shoved" through high school, who will gift him with time and patience; who will answer all of his questions, listen, and offer hope and encouragement. Mark is preparing to write the GED having discovered that his diploma is not accepted for entrance to college because it was not obtained through the general or advanced stream.

John has just recently come to understand that it was not personal limitation that bewildered and overwhelmed him at university. A knowing educator shared not only why his history is new to him but also why the emotions created by the content in his Native studies major were so intense as to exhaust him to the point that he had to leave.

Where do these individuals find the kind of support they need? It can be found in some Native literacy programs.

ASSUMPTIONS

During the course of this research I have been motivated and influenced by my Aboriginal spirituality and worldview. My biases are generated by the teachings of equality and interconnectedness in the medicine wheel. My study of deviations between verb based Aboriginal language and noun based English gives explanation to my impatience with so much "talk and no action" in Native literacy. The uniqueness required in Native literacy has been in print for a long time but there appears to be no avenue to create action. Further, reflective teaching in the Aboriginal community and literacy informs me that Aboriginal relevant "literacy" materials have been requested for the last twenty years and yet they are for the most part still unavailable. A further assumption is that in the Aboriginal community those who could write the materials, the people working in the front lines, are without fail the overworked and underpaid.

Experiences in education created assumptions that education will not empower Aboriginal people. In fact it is very disempowering to a dedicated Aboriginal teacher. This causes me to question the wisdom of sending future generations into institutions of higher learning if young people continue to be denied the spiritual foundation required to cope with the certainty of ethnostress, a condition resulting from years of oppressive experience (Hill 1986). My experiences further inform me that as the Aboriginal individual goes higher in postsecondary education outside control becomes an issue.

My experiences in literacy created the assumptions that: literacy training in Ontario has a very limited scope; statistics are the enemy of Native literacy; policy emanating from the "proverbial ivory tower" of hierarchy continues to deny input from the most important stakeholders, the workers and learners; "Native" literacy perpetuates the use of the English language to misrepresent hope to the Aboriginal population.

CONTRIBUTION OF THIS THESIS TO THE FIELD OF NATIVE LITERACY

These assumptions led me to question why Native literacy is ineffective; what is needed to make Native literacy effective; and what would change the future? My final assumption is that Native literacy needs to be defined by Aboriginal worldview and concepts. In writing my argument for re presenting Native literacy, I have two intentions the first being that clarifying the basis and intent of Native literacy will invite substantial support from governments at all levels including at the local reserve level; the second being that creative solutions in the form of materials will become the focus of funding.

DEFINING TERMS

The **Oxford Dictionary** defines **literacy** as "the ability to read and write" (Elliot, Knight and Cowley 1997) while the **International Adult Literacy Survey** (IALS) defines literacy as "using printed and written information to function in society, to achieve one's goals, and to develop one's knowledge" (Sault College 1997). This thesis uses the **Ministry of Training, Colleges and Universities (MTCU)** definition of literacy "the ability to read, write, calculate, speak, and understand, as well as sign (for the Deaf) and communicate in other forms of language, according to need. Literacy is a continuum, of skills necessary for everyday life in the home, at work, in education, and in the community" (MTCU 2000) to discuss the need to further a more relevant definition to represent Native literacy.

The term **Native literacy** is used by the Ministry of Training, Colleges and Universities (MTCU) to define one of three designated cultural (stream) groups; Francophone, DEAF, and Native (Aboriginal) within Ontario Literacy all of which follow the same policies and whose stream titles simply describe a line item in an accounting mechanism. It is this representation that is disputed in this thesis. In a discussion with an MTCU consultant, I was told that there is no such thing as Native Literacy being different to mean meeting Native needs in an a Native way. It is just a title the same as Francophone, Deaf and Anglophone.

Incorporated since 1988, the **Ontario Native Literacy Coalition (ONLC)** is one of four provincial umbrella literacy groups funded by Ministry of Training, Colleges and Universities (MTCU) to provide provincial networking and to support field development in Native literacy according to MTCU's defining terms (Lepine 2003). In effect, ONLC is an employee of the Ontario Government whose loyalties are governed by the 100% funding through MTCU.

Two related terms – holistic and wholistic - are used in the literature. The term **holistic** designates a non-Aboriginal concept and describes a "holistic philosophy in which the term 'related' is taken as meaning 'all things are interconnected' by virtue of sharing an environment in which action leads to a type of 'domino effect' in a secular world" (Antone, Gamlin and Provost-Turchetti 2003:9).

The term spelled **wholistic** is used to designate the Aboriginal understanding.

"Wholistic" describes the Aboriginal philosophy in which "everything is related" by virtue of shared origins and in which, by extension, the human being is considered an entire whole; that is mentally, physically, spiritually, and emotionally as an individual, with one's family and extended family, one's people, and with the cosmos in sacred relationships (Antone et al 2003:9).

A geographical definition of isolated is used for funding purposes by the department of Indian and Northern Affairs (INAC). INAC considers a community, Zone 4, isolated if there is no year-round road access to government services, banks, health services, community and social services, and suppliers at a service center, which is

defined as the nearest community containing the aforementioned services. (INAC 2004:2, Aboriginal Canada Portal 2003: b, vi). A community may possibly be isolated if in Zone 3, over 350km from the nearest service center with year round access (Duchesne 2005).

This study uses a **philosophical definition of isolated.** Isolated in this paper is defined as without the human support of services provided by people of the same ethnic and cultural group (Monture 1995:173-181; Dupuis 2002:124; Mercredi and Turpel 1993:230; Friere 1985:48-49; Hill 1995:59) and further adopts the "psychic boundaries between oppressors and oppressed" (Friere 1973: x).

RESEARCH QUESTIONS

Entering the field of literacy as a primary education specialist and adult educator gives me the advantage of a repertoire of methodology, knowledge of "gaps" created for the poor by an inflexible formal education system and experience with learning disabilities. Twelve years as principal provided me with a sound training and base for evaluating resources in a program as well as human resources. It is these same advantages that led me to my research questions. I questioned why a resource that must address such basic needs and such large numbers is so poorly funded. When told that literacy programs have no funds for buying books and cannot use their funds to create materials it made no sense when project number one is to increase the ability to read and write. Lastly, the degree of administration required of the program managers takes more time than the manager (who is also the one-to-one tutor) has to work with the learners in a "learner centered" program. Ergo my first research question: What is literacy in its broad definition?

As an Aboriginal grandmother, involved in Native literacy as an instructor and a member of the provincial network, Ontario Native Literacy Coalition (ONLC) board, I balked at restrictive guidelines and often irrelevant directives that Native literacy tries to enforce. I see literacy as a springboard for individual empowerment and community development. Teaching experience informs me that there is a hierarchy of needs to be met before an individual can learn. Native history and education informs me that new needs have been created in the Aboriginal population. Native literacy attempts to repeat the school the experience of its learners in that it follows edicts that deny any form of life-skill training. As a board member for two years and as president of the ONLC for one year the overpowering feeling of being an adversary rather than a proponent of Native literacy grew and created the need to answer the questions: What is Ontario Native Literacy? How is it defined? Limited? Related to literacy?

Wisdom of my parents and grandparents taught me that exposing a problem is only half the project. Finding a solution is part of that same responsibility. Sharing wisdom I have accumulated is also my responsibility and that led me to ask the questions: What is Native wholistic literacy? What more does it encompass? This exercise has increased my motivation to continue my work in Native literacy beyond wanting to help my boss continue her efforts at wholistic literacy while avoiding being marked, "does not meet requirements" in her Ministry monitoring visit.

My Connection to These Questions

This research was born out of frustration with the overly confining rules and lack of resources in Ontario literacy. The same rules and lack of funding prevent Native literacy practitioners from practicing wholistic literacy for their specific needs.

Forced from the formal education system (twenty-six years teaching at the primary/junior level, twelve as principal at two different Aboriginal community schools) for lack of "proper training", I began attending university full time in 2000. I now hold a degree in Native Studies and this research is a partial fulfillment of a master's degree in Sociology and Equity Studies in Education at the Ontario Institute of Studies in Education (OISE/UT). I do not qualify for OSAP because I own a house – mortgaged, but it puts me out of range of an Ontario student loan. There is no consideration for mature students who for a variety of reason have to return to school fulltime.

Procuring a part-time job tutoring in a Native literacy program I initially questioned my fit because adult literacy sounded very different from my experience even though I had completed my twentieth year teaching Methods in a Native Classroom Assistant summer program (NCADP) at Nipissing University North Bay. What I found in adult literacy were the individuals who hadn't gained sufficient education for even the classroom assistant program (grade eight to ten). More noteworthy however, is the fact that most of the individuals I work with in adult literacy had been labeled either "a behaviour problem" or "learning disabled" during their childhood and adolescent schooling and have either been accelerated out of high-school or dropped out. When I tutor them we discover that most are not dyslexic; many simply have a learning style that was not accommodated. In hindsight, it occurs to me that I seem to be the only literacy worker with the audacity to insist on asking why? No doubt it is the Aboriginal teacher in me.

After four years working in adult literacy I know that the government is in total control not only of funding but policy as well; a hierarchal system prohibits front line workers doing the job they know needs done; no one can state precisely what literacy is; ministry policy happens despite the input of learners and practitioners; the real human successes can not be recorded in the stats; while there is an abundance of government administrators and officials, the programs must depend on volunteers.

Additionally, my position as president of the Ontario Native Literacy Coalition (ONLC) has been illuminating. As a board member and president of ONLC I attended several meetings with Ministry of Training, Colleges and Universities (MTCU). The political belief and attitude; "we are the experts, we are the funders and we enforce policies based on statistics", are strong and impenetrable. Educated by a euro-western, patriarchal and hierarchal system, MTCU officials and its literacy consultants have been educated to accept the status quo as has the Aboriginal population. The worldview is naturalized by education and other institutions. For Native people the imposition of this worldview has created its own form of internal stress expressed in a variety of violence.

Experience in formal education and literacy led me to research a definition of literacy in general in order to articulate a definition of Native literacy that can be used to meet the needs of Aboriginal people. For the individuals previously described, literacy programs are the last resort and the literacy experience cannot be a repeat of their prior school experience otherwise dismal results will be repeated. The "Canadian version" of genocide – cultural and numeric - has created a unique education process that buries the truth of the post contact origins of dysfunction in the Aboriginal community. This unhealthy conditioning of Aboriginal individuals needs to be addressed. Wholistic Native literacy based on Aboriginal worldview will begin that process.

STRUCTURE OF THE THESIS

Chapter one presents the context of the research questions and while definition of wholistic Native literacy is the purpose of this thesis, it is necessary in chapter two to clarify the confusion of Native literacy not being "Native". My attendance at several Native literacy gatherings, MTCU monitoring visits and the literacy Symposium at OISE in 2003, have awakened me to this much needed understanding in the Aboriginal community.

Chapter two then presents a brief historical background to Ontario literacy, policy that drives it, and administration that monitors it.

Chapter three relates Native literacy in the context of Ontario Literacy. The chapter describes the incongruity of "Native" literacy in the Aboriginal community. The chapter will clarify to the reader the need to re present Native literacy.

Chapter four begins by presenting original Aboriginal worldview as it relates to Native wholistic literacy. An argument for the redefinition of Native literacy is based in the intergenerational trauma of Canadian Aboriginal history. Wholistic literacy in the Aboriginal sense is presented as well as a vision of the possible impacts on the Aboriginal community should it be implemented.

Chapter five summarizes and the conclusion recaps the research and leaves the reader with a view of the proverbial "ripple effect" of one small change in the waters of Native literacy. The intention is to open doors that have been closed to possibilities for Aboriginal peoples; doors that Native literacy as dictated by Ontario literacy continues to keep closed.

CHAPTER 2

ONTARIO LITERACY:
LITERACY FOR LIBERATION OR
LITERACY FOR CONFORMITY?

Literacy has become a prominent issue in Canada. Statistics taken from the International Adult Literacy Survey (IALS) report a high percentage of Canadians (38%) with literacy levels sufficiently low enough to thwart employment. Chapter two will document the progress and direction that Ontario has taken to deal with its illiteracy problem. A very brief overall history of literacy in Canada introduces the development of Ontario literacy.

Literacy has changed since the 1970s when it was first recognized as an inability to read or to write. According to Doug Anderson, former literacy practitioner and current business planner of the new National Indigenous Literacy Association (NILA) in its origins literacy was offered by volunteers around kitchen tables for those who had not had the opportunity to go to school (Anderson 2003). As the extent of literacy need was exposed, a more formal delivery was developed and literacy providers became colleges, school boards and community based agencies. In 1986, the Ministry of Education and Training in Ontario undertook the responsibility of administering adult literacy (Harwood 2001) implementing Literacy and Basic Skills in 1999 (Ministry of Education 2001). The National Literacy Secretariat (NLS) was created in 1987 to support national and provincial literacy organizations. During the process the voluntary and lifestyle -changing atmosphere of the original concept of literacy training changed. To understand the scope of

Ontario literacy and its relationship to Native literacy in Ontario, it is necessary to contemplate literacy policy and procedure.

The Literacy and Basic Skills Guidelines 2000, provides definitions that clarify Ontario literacy program reform that "streamlined program delivery, made it more cost efficient and better focused on learner's needs, such as assistance in finding employment" (Ministry of Training, Colleges and Universities 2000). In Ontario, the Ministry of Training, Colleges and Universities (MTCU), through the Literacy and Basic Skills (LBS) Program is responsible for funding and supporting quality adult literacy services through **LBS Programs** (MTCU 2000). **Basic Skills** are borrowed from the *Essential Skills Project* by Human Resources Skills Development Canada (HRSDC). Basic reading, writing and numeracy skills are embedded in the literacy outcomes: basic computer skills, continuous learning, decision making, finding information, numeracy, planning and organizing, problem-solving, and working with others. **Learners** are the individuals who are enrolled in training, adults who are at least nineteen, out of school and do not have the literacy skills necessary to meet their needs, as measured by levels one and two of the international survey. **Contact Hours** include only the actual time spent directly involved, face to face with the learner. Leaner time spent using a computer and learning software is not included, nor is homework. Nor is administration included although continued funding is based on meeting the assigned contact hours. **AlphaPlus Center** is one of three service organizations funded by the Ministry of Training, Colleges and Universities. AlphaPlus Centre is funded to provide library services, technology services, information on literacy projects, and access to discussions with providers and other literacy professionals. (MTU 2000)

LBS service development infrastructure includes four **Sectoral Bodies** which provide service to delivery agencies that share a distinctive approach to literacy; colleges, school boards, and two community based organizations Literacy Ontario and Laubach Literacy Ontario (MTCU 2000). **Streams** to ensure that the literacy needs of learners from different linguistic and cultural backgrounds are addressed are recognized through Literacy and Basic Skills. The four literacy steams are Anglophone, Deaf (G.O.L.D.), Francophone and Native. Sixteen support **Networks** defined by geographical regions meet the networking needs of LBS Anglophone delivery agencies throughout Ontario. The networks assist in the Ontario literacy marketing strategy. **Umbrella groups** include the sixteen regional networks as well as Anglophone, Francophone, GOLD and Native stream coalitions (D'Arville 1992).

Learner assessment based on the Learning Outcomes Matrix places the learner at one of five levels indicating a beginning level of programming (Stat Can 1996). **Level 1** indicates very low literacy skills, where the individual may, for example, have difficulty identifying the correct medicine to give a child from the information found on the package. **Level 2** respondents can deal with material that is simple, clearly laid out and in which the tasks involved are not too complex. This is a significant category, because it identifies people who may have adapted their lower literacy skills to everyday life, but would have difficulty learning new job skills requiring a higher level of literacy. **Level 3** is considered as the minimum desirable threshold. **Levels 4 and 5** indicate higher literacy skills requiring the ability to integrate several sources of information or solve more complex problems.

A **Practitioner** is the individual who has accepted the responsibility for administering and delivering literacy training in an LBS program. In a stand-alone program this individual is in essence, the principal, instructor, janitor, fundraiser, bookkeeper and accountant for the program and operates with the guidance of a volunteer board. Without significant fundraising the practitioner is the sole paid staff of the program. The most recent controversy in literacy is the Workplace/Workforce Initiative. **Workforce literacy** is defined as LBS delivery agencies using methodologies and materials relevant to learners who have employment goals. **Workplace literacy** is the provision of LBS-like services to a specific workplace.

HISTORY AND DEVELOPMENT OF ONTARIO LITERACY

"Literacy boundaries in social life go back several centuries. Ever since colonial explorers made it their *mission civilatrice* to bring imperial culture and education to poor, uncivilized, ignorant, and illiterate "savages" around the world, there have existed political, cultural, moral, and instructional dimensions to the provision of literacy" (Venezky, Wagner, Ciliberte 1990). In many ways this statement explains the discrepancy between what government dictates and what practitioners and literacy learners need. In his article, *Literacy for What Purpose?*, Larry Mikulecky comments that a decade of research in literacy demonstrates three major points about its delivery: "literacy processes vary widely to reflect the pluralism of social contexts in which literacy is used and transfer of literacy abilities is severely limited by differences in format, social support networks, and required background information as one moves from context to context" (Venezky, Wagner, Ciliberte 1990). In Ontario literacy it appears that the colonial attitude blocks the acceptance that diversity is paramount in literacy. A "one size fits all" style of service prevails. Further, the foregoing statements serve to explain the apparent wall of indifference that literacy practitioners confront daily in on-going communications with MTCU Literacy officials regarding learner goals and overly time-consuming administration. Despite anything practitioners say, they are continually in a position of promoting policy that often defeats the literacy learner from the outset. "Literacy benchmarks and practices [that] address the important objectives of improved accountability to the public and the development of quality standards" (MTCU 1995), are incompatible not only with the resources available but also with the reality of poverty and government oppression at the grassroots level. Who exactly is the public? One would have thought that the learners are part of that population yet services, programs and delivery designed to appease the public alienate the learner from any hope of a change in their standard of living. This statement clearly leaves out the hopes and aspirations of the learner.

In 2005, Ontario literacy continues to lose its empowerment focus under government guise of accountability. Despite the claim that reform of the LBS program "has established balance of accountability and customer service" (MTCU 2000), the emphasis of literacy training is now employability. This leaves those in the field to accept that MTCU has ignored input from practitioners who have stated time and again that the majority of learners at level one and two don't arrive in basic literacy programs with an employment goal (HRDC 2000, Horsman 2000). The fact that "the government of Ontario has identified literacy and basic skills as an essential element in its economic development strategy" (MTCU 2000) is rapidly overpowering the sense of social change and notions of literacy creating equity, which was the original focus of literacy. Until 2000, literacy learners were offered non-threatening, voluntary, one-to-one tutoring to meet the goals they had set for themselves, employment, education/training or independence, as per LBS guidelines (MTCU 2000). Now learners must incorporate employment goals into their learning path while their intelligence informs them that: social assistance/Ontario Works (OW) at a minimum provides some avenue to improve while a menial job does not and that their family is at greater risk of becoming homeless with a low paying job. When a learner expresses an employment goal a time limit appears, social development and further education and training are ignored and the learner is exited from literacy to an employment agency as quickly as possible and here there is a significant disconnect between what the learner can do and what the agency sends them to. Learners are caught in a system that failed them originally yet is now forcing them to take a job that creates a distinct possibility of downward, not upward mobility from living on social assistance.

At the administration level the commitment to literacy training appears to have dwindled to a field of research while the administrators have distanced themselves from the LBS delivery program. Surveys and meetings with MTCU indicate that policy is set before the practitioner has input. On-line discussions are opened for practitioner input only after policy is already written[1]. My experience with methodological guidelines and asking good research questions at Trent University and University of Toronto leads me to

---

1 I have participated in three such surveys on-line at AlphaPlus as well as open discussions on the internet over a four year period. As ONLC board member I have participated in the collection of surveys and have critiqued and experienced the way they are conducted.

believe that MTCU questionnaires and surveys, research that leads to policy, would not get through an ethics committee because they are guilty of framing the question to lead the answer.

The *Taking Stock of Literacy and Basic Skills Capacity to Serve Learners with Employment Goals* is an excellent example of how MTCU influenced data to fit their agenda. This heavily skewed survey had to be attached as part of the 2004/2005 LBS Program business plan. "Question #1 Do you offer LBS services to learners with employment-related learning goals"? Question #1c If you answered No to question 1, is there an LBS Program in your community to which you are able to refer learners with employment related learning goals ? Yes or No The remainder of the six page survey offers opportunity to choose the employment sector your learners most frequently indicate interest in, indicate on a scale from 1 to 5 how your agency would benefit from Professional Development opportunities related to working with learners with employment goals, and prioritize Professional Development to increase your capacity to more effectively serve learners with employment goals.

The results of this survey were statistics geared to employment goals, used to justify the millions of dollars spent on Train Ontario, training workshops to familiarize the literacy field with workforce literacy, out of a literacy budget of $60 million and provide statistics to influence the Ministry to be inflexible on learner goals. Several other initiatives named Program Reform, Common Assessment, and Learner Satisfaction were implemented in much the same way - all supporting employment exclusive of self-development. MTCU references the Taking Stock Survey as the impetus for Train Ontario – Workforce/Workplace literacy policy.

LBS program practitioners are often stressed under the intolerance shown by MTCU when employment goals are not the norm. While it is literacy for the Workplace that contains the statement, "LBS services are expected to focus on the employment and employability needs of their clients, so that the literacy skills learned will help clients find a job, keep a job they have in a changing work environment, or be able to acquire positions with greater skills demands." (MTCU 2000) LBS programs are not workplaces yet employment is being forced into basic literacy programs as the paramount goal. Despite three goal paths for literacy learners: employment; training/education; and independence, it appears that only employment is an acceptable option. (Monitoring visit 2005)

The intolerance appears during monitoring visits as well as through the Train Ontario Phase II survey. An example given in Phase II Train Ontario, of how employment goals are promoted by one LBS Program stated that the practitioner "makes" the learner consider an employment goal when they don't have one. Research indicates that learners at levels one and two understand that level three, and often four and five will not provide them with access to employment (Haley and Davidson 2000, NAPO 1992). Current Ontario Works (OW) mandatory literacy testing sends learners to literacy who not only can't see their way clear to academically accessing higher education but who are unable to access sufficient funding to support their move to higher learner and training. In my personal experience these learners fill programs to capacity, creating added administration demands, because many don't want to be there, attend sporadically and leave. Some who are in between jobs are sent according to policy, create administration and leave as soon as they find another job.

Our experience at the agency level is that the norm is to lose learners to more immediate financial issues. Learners are not leaving LBS Programs to employment as the Taking Stock 2003 statistics have been skewed to reveal. They leave because they cannot afford child care and transportation, as well as food and clothing for their family. One person sick in the family has the effect of either creating a family epidemic because of insufficient funds for common medicinal treatments or literally taking food from the table. (Personal experience with learners) To reduce the deficit and save taxpayers money, Canada cut funding for housing increasing the likelihood of more homelessness. Individuals and families "either on income assistance or working for low wages" frequently find that a miniscule change in their situation can put them on the homeless list (Hargrave 2004).

LBS programs have a history of difficulty attracting and keeping learners due to stigma attached to "illiteracy" which at one point was considered "special ed" for adults (Veeman 2002, Darville 1992). Constant emphasis on employment training only serves to highlight a very long road ahead and demoralizes the learner before the practitioner has the opportunity to get him/her motivated to continue. In the aftermath of these methods the most important stakeholders, the learners and those frontline workers who put their whole being into trying to ameliorate personal damage done by Ontario institutions, are left with policy that imposes an employment training focus where it simply cannot be effective, in an LBS Program that can only take the learner to a level three. An assessment of level four or five would have the learner sent to an Ontario Basic Skills (OBS) at a college (MTCU 2000).

There appears to be abundant funding for infrastructure, but very little funding for the actual program work that needs to be done. Sixteen Networks, three service organizations, and MTCU decisions without consultation are funded in the hundreds of thousands of dollars yet the average LBS program receives fifty thousand per year. An example of the "stinginess at program level" (Darville 1992) can be found in the funding our program was given for Workforce Training materials in winter, 2005 which amounted to well under $1000 dollars and had to be spent on Workforce Literacy materials. Also in winter, 2005 hundreds of thousands of dollars are extended to research through MTCU/ NLS projects. In fact, Literacy practitioners who have hardly delivered the workforce training and have not yet caught their breath after business plan submission and winter, 2005 program monitoring visits, were being informed by a letter dated March 2, 2005, that they may be involved in "Learner Skill Attainment" research to "enhance the recognition of learner attainment and the accountability of the LBS Program". More accountability! One would think that there is more than one paid staff in the programs.

Research is the focus of the National Literacy Secretariat (NLS) and research dollars are aimed at "increasing the research capacity of the Canadian literacy community, supporting increased quality in literacy research in Canada, diminishing the separation of research and practice, and ensuring stakeholders can access the research-based knowledge they need" (HRSDC 2005). While project funding can be accessed for: developing materials, researching literacy needs; improving access to literacy programs and outreach; improving co-ordination and information sharing; and increasing public awareness (HRSDC 2005), the bulk of the funding will go to service organizations such as AlphaPlus Center and Ningwakwe Learning Press, organizations far removed from the day to day, one-to-one activities of an LBS Program. Then again, very few practitioners are inclined to add research to their daily struggle or to participate in research.

The AlphaPlus Centre, supplier of technical security to the entire field appears to receive the bulk of the dollars. For example, AlphaPlus Center received "$419,000 out of $2,000,000 to strengthen literacy training for job creation and economic growth" (Ministry of Education/ Ministry of Training, Colleges and Universities November 2001).

A little known fact that support comes only in the form of software training not continuing technological assistance for a project, changes the presentation of AlphaPlus as the technology lifesaver of isolated practitioners. In fact the practitioner involved had to withdraw funding designated for support from AlphaPlus to "hire" other technicians to help with the completion of the project. In many ways the MTCU person assigned to critique, award and support projects and the AlphaPlus center failed this community program practitioner. A threat of getting "written up" when the practitioner requested more money or paring down of the project to make it work [2] appears more appropriate for a primary school child. This kind of activity demoralizes the practitioner who dares to bring their community "grassroots" experience and knowledge of community and individual needs to the aid of other practitioners (Horsman 1999, Darville 1992).

---

2 I was the program support person for the project. My hours in the LBS program were extended to accommodate this.

WHATEVER HAPPENED TO "COMMUNITY" IN COMMUNITY PROGRAMS?

Richard Darville's statement "community is a cousin of privatization" in *Adult Literacy Work in Canada* answers at least one of several questions that prompted this research: how the same government that controls formal education institutions can seemingly deny a relationship between literacy and schooling. How much equity is there when learners in literacy programs, individuals failed by education and society, are assigned to the margins with so little funding, to assist them (ABC Canada 2002)? Many learners are in their situation because of a learning disability and have been "pushed through" (words of the learners) institutions with special education funding, by teachers with degrees. They are forced into literacy programs with sincere community people who are not teachers with degrees to teach them. How can government excuse the mere average of $50,000/year/program that is offered to programs? (Personal communications with practitioners)

"An important measure of schooling's success is literacy. Levels of literacy skills provide a measure of how students are prepared to participate in the Canadian knowledge-based economy. Differences in literacy skills among students with differing family backgrounds and characteristics also indicate whether schools are providing students with equitable opportunities" (Fallis 1998). Experiences working one on one with learners in literacy over a four year period and experience working with Aboriginal adults over a twenty year period indicate that equitable opportunities have not been provided for the poor, ethnic, rural and learning disabled in the formal school system. The numbers of individuals who "fell through the cracks" of the formal education system can be identified as the 68,000 individuals who are attending a literacy program. (ME/MTCU 2001) This population can be found in the numbers of individuals on Social Assistance (Ontario Works). It begs the question - how many of the population living in poverty, 1, 378,300 in 1994 according to the Canadian Council on Social Development fact sheets live

on social assistance and have literacy issues. http://www.ccsd.ca/
factsheets/welf395.html

"Today's increasing tendency to view literacy as primarily an
economic issue raises questions of whether literacy for social equity
and democracy, and literacy for economic productivity can remain
aligned" (Weinstein and Lewis 1998). In my conversations at
meetings, in programs and on-line discussions many practitioners
express their fear that the economic focus has dominated, leaving them
unsatisfied in their work. Rapid turnover in the field is a reality that
appears to be creating an atmosphere of instability. Long-standing
practitioners, who have been involved with the growth of literacy
from the field's infancy, are leaving. For many, the stress of workforce
literacy and the increased degree of administration have erased the
attraction to literacy (Lepine 2003). They no longer experience
the drive to advocate for the learner in this mercenary accounting
atmosphere. Many entered the field motivated by a humanitarian
attitude. More than one practitioner has left with the statement,
"I'm so tired of fighting a losing battle!" At the meetings I attend
and at literacy programs, practitioners can be heard questioning their
participation in current administration dominated literacy. Perhaps a
lack of continuity is the intent of MTCU initiatives. With continued
adherence to this trend eventually few will remember the original
spirit of literacy. Additionally, the learner in a learner-centered
program can be legitimately ignored. Colonialism continues in
2005. The privileged, the government and its officials, continue to
maintain control over the poor, the practitioners and the learners,
through policy that ensures a large class of people to dominate.

To me a former teacher, it sounds a lot like the Harris "Common
Sense" regime, a period of time in which Harris was premier of
Ontario and substantially cut educational funding. During this time
many sincere, dedicated teachers who would argue against the new
education policy for the sake of "the kids" were demoralized and left
the profession. In my case, child development and integrity were
important and I could not continue to fight a losing battle against
government and parents who had been wholistically conditioned
to believe that governments know best. Despite the discrepancy

between Ontario Government use of holistic and Aboriginal wholistic concept, further addressed in chapter three, government has used wholistic means to program a large population who live in poverty to believe that they are inferior and so incapable as to have no rights. Experience working with urban Ontario Works clients and Aboriginal welfare clients very quickly exposes the tyranny that controls medical, dental, nutrition, living conditions, self-esteem and futures of such a large Ontario population. The Aboriginal population must deal also with white privilege.

The new Workforce literacy strategy introduced in Ontario in 2001 began its visioning in 1995 (Belfore 2002). In fact, Workplace education began in the70s and 80s (Belfore 2002:2). I wonder if anyone contemplated the pervasive influence the Workforce Investment Act of 1998 would have over Literacy and Basic Skills (LBS) programming or the amount of funding that would go into Workforce Literacy in Ontario to the detriment of individual programs. Considering that "Ontario residents whose literacy skills fall within levels one and two of the International Literacy Survey (IALS) are the primary focus of the program (LBS Guidelines 2000) " it begs the question; "How can basic literacy programs be held responsible for getting this population employment ready?"

In 2004, all Ontario literacy programs were mandated to attend workshops that would train them to "demonstrate their effectiveness. [Programs] are expected to focus on the employment and employability needs of their clients so that the literacy skills learned will help their clients find a job, keep the job they have in a changing work environment, or be able to acquire positions with greater skill demands." These words can be found in the script of MTCU consultants who presented the Ministry of Training Colleges and Universities message at each of the trainings. In a further section of the message, "MTCU recognized that employment may not be the goal of every learner who enters an LBS agency." However, all training and funding is exclusively for workforce development. MTCU recognized that it is not possible for all LBS learners who develop their skills and their employability to gain employment, due to barriers such as societal discrimination, local economic conditions and high unemployment rates, or lack of grade twelve credentials." Despite this acknowledgement Train Ontario Phase II was training practitioners to manipulate learners to pursue an employment goal. In their Learning Works message they state, "The purpose of this training is not to address these broader societal issues, although as a practitioner that is the context in which you and your learners live and learn." Government acknowledges the barriers practitioners have articulated but persist in pushing its agenda – accountability- for what? by whom? Perhaps the accountability requires closer monitoring of funded employment planning agencies. In my experience these employment agencies impose administration fee claw backs that make leaving social assistance for employment unrealistic even for the learners who get their grade twelve equivalency. The worker gets minimum wage portion of the pay, the agency takes the rest with no apparent consideration that the learner has no transportation, wardrobe, or employment necessities. In fact, my experience in Peterborough and Toronto tells me that depending on the region one lives in, Ontario Works only contemplates employment at the end of GED and the individual must fight for further education.

LITERACY FUNDING: ACCOUNTABILITY V.S. THE LEARNER

Program funding falls under the following funding variables: quality of service and results achieved as demonstrated by past performance; compliance with LBS guidelines; projected activity levels expressed as numbers of contact hours; business plan that reflects the literacy services plan; participation in the local planning and coordination process; historic activity and funding levels; geography (urban/ small town/rural); accessibility of services to clients and learners; proximity to like services or need for stand-alone services; labour market pressures; growth or rationalization of the agency or its services; access to library, labs etc." (MTCU 2000:7). Funding for literacy programs has not increased since Program Reform in 1999.

In my pursuit of accommodation for time spent on administration in June 2004, the response from Ministry of Training, Colleges and

Universities was, "Funding will stay the same. Service demands have increased. You can only do what you can do with what you've got". I responded, "in other words there are some services that will have to either be lessened or dropped". I didn't receive a yes or no answer, just a repeat of "You can only do what you can with what you've got". The message I took and forwarded to the practitioners was that practitioners could lessen their unfunded outside activities (LSP meetings). Monitoring visits gave a resounding "no". It is very easy to earn a "doesn't meet requirements" in a monitoring visit and not attending LSP meetings results in losing one of those fourteen out of seventeen required check marks (MTCU 2004). How did the learner in a "learner centered" system become less important than ministry accountability? MTCU categorically refused to acknowledge the growing amount of administration.

Michael Bach (2000) of the Roeher Institute contributes "when literacy is defined as a skill it is difficult to argue that literacy is a human right. People cannot have a right to a particular skill but they do have a right to participate in processes and institutions like democracy, justice and education." Even though there is no absolute definition of literacy and while there is a lot of literature that contemplates literacy as a social justice issue, the narrow one that Ontario enforces does not consider this broader definition.

Further, "by defining literacy as a skill, the responsibility for the lack of literacy is placed squarely on the shoulders of the individual who is deemed deficient" (Bach 2000). Literacy as a right would put the responsibility back on to the education system. During the program reform years, skills training replaced literacy as a right.

Bach goes on to say that considering the "numerous studies that point to a crisis in literacy and considering that so many resources have been invested in literacy producing very little change, perhaps the concept of how the communication is written should be addressed (Bach 2000)". Not only is the amount of research written about literacy daunting to that literacy worker with all the administration, but also the language used is most certainly not written for the literacy practitioner. It is written in language only another researcher can decipher and more than that, it is about something the practitioner already knows through personal experience or experience working one to one with learners. The fact that it is not known by a researcher, written by a researcher or produced by a researcher appears to invalidate it. Further, terminology and language that grassroots workers have learned in their isolation from academia must be replaced by language that academic researchers coin. This exercise alone creates "controversy" in the literacy field. It reminds me of my own experience.

I owned and managed a small business in a small town. The bookkeeping and accounting were my responsibility and after four years of preparing for the income tax and year-end I became quite proficient and saved the business hundreds of dollars at the chartered accountant's office every year. In the fifth year I went to college for a course in general accounting. I came near to dropping out of the course. Putting their labels and constraints on practices I had been doing was very hard and time consuming and I had to know them in order to pass the exams. In other words I almost failed something I knew because I could not make it fit within the academic frame. Practitioners do not get the time to digest research rhetoric. They limp along, doing their best, mechanically filling in surveys and questionnaires finding out too late that their responses have created "statistics".

It is time to provide funding for the monumental work needed that research continually exposes (Veeman 2002, Venezky 1992, ABC Canada, Canadian Education Association 2004, Fallis 1998, and Horsman 1999). Literacy needs more paid staff with materials and books owned on site. Practitioners need more supportive people in administration. Practitioners need more recognition and rewards for their efforts.

During the winter of 2004 I participated in an on-line discussion of the International Adult Literacy Survey (IALS), the much-touted document that now steers literacy policy. When a rising concern over skills training replacing literacy training was discussed, it validated practitioners who had been stating that important elements of literacy work are hard to get done anymore due to reporting and funding requirements rigidly focused on increasing skill levels.

In that same winter of 2004 discussion, Nayda Veeman, Graduate Student of University of Saskatchewan and Research Collaborator, raised the point that possibly a simple rule of giving " priority in adult education spending to those with the least education, no matter the colour or race" would better serve literacy efforts than relegating them to unskilled teachers and volunteers. Over the course of this research I have read this same thought in many reports from literacy conferences (Bossort 1990; Antone 2003; Darville 1992). However, there is a danger in this thought. It could lead to policy that literacy practitioners and workers would have to be certified. One only has to interview older retired teachers and principals to find out the effect of prescripted over education. A five-year university requirement does not a better teacher make! For example, in the Aboriginal world, the prescripted requirement to certify Native language teachers has served to alienate communities from their own language and in fact has forced anglicized methodology, which further impedes the revitalization of Native language.[3] Practitioners work with a broad range of students in all levels one to three! In my experience they need some training in disabilities, foundational math and language acquisition methods. They do not have time or energy left to attend courses that will not ease their daily work.

Practitioners will tell you it is not the certification that is needed, it is "home grown" materials, better pay, and more staff. Practitioners are seeking training to recognize and accommodate learning disabilities. The training is not coming through MTCU despite research reports OLC 2001, and delivery agencies are left to seek the training for them selves.

---

3 I have witnessed this effect in my home community. My father is one of the casualties. His first language is Ojibway. He was punished for speaking it at school as a child. He refused to teach his children the language so that they wouldn't be punished. When I was the principal in the school he again refused to teach the language stating that they (meaning the certified language teachers from Lakehead University) were teaching the right Ojibway! During the summer course I teach at Nipissing University my students from reserves all over Ontario speak of the same experience in their communities. There is an Aboriginal term, "Ojiberish," used in the Ojibway community to describe the results of the certified language teachers' teaching.

Objectives of Literacy and
Basic Skills Programs

Through the Literacy and Basic Skills Program, the Ministry of Education/Ministry of Training Colleges and Universities funds Ontario agencies to provide literacy services (MTCU 2000:1). Following are the "Objectives of the Literacy and Basic Skills Program (LBS)": 1. to help Ontario move towards a seamless adult education system that supports **lifelong learning** 2. To support literacy agencies in providing **quality** literacy services that meet learner needs 3. To focus literacy services on those adults **most in need** of them 4. To ensure **accountability** to government, to the public, and to learners in the provision of literacy services that are effective, efficient, and produce measurable results 5. To foster closer links between literacy training and **employment** (MTCU 2000). The five objectives of literacy basic skills will serve as an organizational tool for this next section that describes the daily administration of an LBS program.

Lifelong Learning

"No longer is it enough for an individual to obtain a skill set through the formal education system. There is now a recognized need that everyone must continue learning throughout his or her lifetime hence the concept of lifelong learning" (Veeman 2002).

Jobs are no longer available to individuals with a grade eight. A few of those who voluntarily arrive at literacy are intent on getting at least a grade twelve equivalency to have a minimum chance at a job but the majority are in search of a better chance by seeking higher education. It has become a common situation to access the General Educational Development (GED) testing service rather than go to upgrading at a College which many individuals state is too slow and complicated by funding issues. Students who are up grading at the college level, levels 4 and 5, cannot access the Ontario Student Assistance Program (OSAP) to offset student living when there is a family concerned.

QUALITY SERVICE

A lot of infrastructure to ensure quality of service exists. There are three levels of bureaucracy above the community literacy program; Umbrella Organizations & Sectoral Bodies; Regional Networks; and MTCU officials and consultants all of whom are responsible for enforcing ministry policy and initiatives. However, they appear to be ensuring their quality of service not the service to the customer[4], the learner. The top heavy funding and miniscule funding and control at the grassroots level expose this. Perhaps this is an explanation for the confusion in literacy policy; policy that contradicts itself in learner centered programs.

This bureaucracy creates the illusion of the capitalist society of "bourgeoisie" and "proletariat" that Karl Marx identified in his manuscripts published in the 1930s. Or is it an illusion? It seems that Marx's concept of "alienation" - the wageworkers lack of control over the production and disposal of his or her product i.e. time and labour is working here (Marshall 1998:391-395). Those at the top not only earn many more times the rate of the frontline worker but they are also the policy makers. They do not meet the learner in the learner's context nor the practitioner. Quality service then is questionable when policy is created based solely on academic research and by individuals who apparently choose not to understand the daily needs and barriers of their customers. This situation puts into question, "learner-centered program".

LEARNER CENTERED FOR LEARNERS MOST IN NEED

Literacy Ontario follows basic formal education language and concepts as required in the Learning Outcomes Matrix and is adamant that they pursue learner centered philosophy. Would this learner centered philosophy mean the same thing as what B.B. Gillani presents: "a student centered curriculum where students can become adept to collaborate, find, analyze, organize, evaluate and internalize new information in light of their own needs based on

---

4 MTCU word used in the terms of reference of the contracts

their academic and cultural backgrounds" (Gillani 1994:4)? Policy indicates it is not.

During monitoring visits practitioners are expected to show how learner goals are directed by the learner; how choice of program is being guided by the learner; how short term goals are "demonstrated" and documented as having been met; and how learners have met their goals before leaving the program. However, only the control is assigned to the learner. The content is controlled by MTCU. Evidently, "evaluate and internalize new information in light of their own needs based on their academic and cultural background" does not factor into it. Adding to the frustration – materials are only available through AlphaPlus on a lending basis. Programs get no money to purchase. Without accessibility to a wide variety of books and materials learners' worlds remain confined to what they know unless the practitioner takes the lead and for this the practitioner can lose those valuable check marks at the monitoring visit.

Furthermore, practitioners reveal that often the needs of the learner are so basic they need time to trust that the practitioner will bear with them (Venezky 1992). Their experience is: to be told what to do; punished for non-compliance; to be text-book learners. They bring all of their negative school conditioning to the LBS program (Haley and Davidson 2000, and Horsman 1999). "Learner centered" is too stressful and if strongly pursued the learner leaves. These concerns are heard every year at "Umbrella" meetings between the four literacy streams and MTCU. Practitioners have been voicing the psychological baggage that learners arrive with that makes it imperative to meet the need of dependency and support in the beginning (Horsman 1999). MTCU's response is,

"Learner directed is your mandate. It is what you agree to in your work plan". Reporting and monitoring visits demand it but is it learner-centered?

Gillani discusses another concept that is of considerable concern to the practitioner both in terms of self and the learner. "Traditional education never considered the concept that human kind has the ability to create more information than individuals can absorb." (Gillani 1994:3) Gillani discusses "information overload" in terms of web-based learning. When MTCU persists in promoting computer based learning to the literacy field perhaps Gillani's concern could be used to protect learners whose first need is self-development and comfort with the notion that they are capable of learning and practitioners with no resources; time, material or human. Small programs struggle to attract and keep learners, and stay current with administration. They don't have time to raise funds to upgrade or buy computers that rapidly become outdated.

Computers are not common among the learners who are sent to literacy through OW and they make up the highest percentage of learners. Further, even if they can access a home computer internet is a non issue. Most learners barely have food on the table (Etkin 1991:224, Lamontagne 2004, Minister of Supply and Services 1996:3, Beauchesne 2005). It would appear that there is a major discrepancy between what the officials "know" literacy learners need and what literacy learners and practitioners know they need.

For many learners, if they decide to make the best of their "prescripted" time in literacy as per the enforced literacy assessment (O. Reg. 417/04) they are more interested in preparing to write the GED for their grade twelve equivalency. Their reasoning is that it is quicker. My personal reflection is that they feel more secure with a "book" because they have been conditioned during their formal education to go from front to back in numerical order and they can see their progress. Jenny Horsman explains it in terms of learner need for control after a history of violence and trauma (Horsman 1999). My experience is that it takes only a short time to convince the learner otherwise. Effective teaching and independent learning cannot take place under this tyranny. "Gaps" that have been created by poor attendance, learning difficulties or disabilities have most often been created in the early years of formal education. These can be identified by beginning at elementary concepts but an adult will often learn the concepts much quicker and there is often no need to complete a whole book, unit or even a page.

ACCOUNTABILITY: POLITICAL

This research uncovered several realities in terms of accountability: accountability leans mostly to government (Sussman 2003); surveys and questionnaires for practitioner input such as during program reform , common assessment, learner exit survey, and workforce needs assessment are heavily skewed to represent government agenda often making it seem that the frontline workers have no worth (Sussman 2003); learners are touted as the real purpose of literacy training yet OW clients have been mandated to do a literacy assessment with the intention of increasing their employability (O. Reg. 417/04) even if their interest is only in helping their children with homework or they are seasonal workers. At www.welfarewatch.toronto.on.ca (17 October 2004), a statement can be found regarding welfare reform in Ontario. "Bill 142, the Social Assistance Reform Act gives new meaning to the provincial government's goal of getting out of the social program business". The Ontario Works Act, 1997 states the legislation "provides temporary financial assistance to those most in need while they satisfy obligations to become and stay employed." As a literacy instructor it has been my experience that those "obligations" create such barriers for the learner invariably they leave literacy.

Individual programs sign funding agreements, which include strict "contact hour" guidelines that control their funding, which hasn't increased since 1988. The LBS Program focuses on adults who are unemployed, with special emphasis on people receiving social assistance and those who are employed and need to improve their skills (MTCU 2000:7). A learner must be without the literacy skills necessary to find and keep a job or meet everyday needs, at least nineteen years old and out of school (MTCU 2000). If this is the "ticket" into a literacy program how can literacy be assigned the accountability requirement of employment goals?

In addition, practitioners are burdened with an extensive statistical and financial reporting system that operates through a computer program titled Information Management Systems. (IMS) Each program must input data regarding learners, training programs, contact hours, etc. each month. The main "hub" of the system operates through AlphaPlus Centre an extravagantly funded support agency. All contact and dissemination of Literacy material happens through AlphaPlus Center. Too often, practitioners cannot "get on". In all sectors of the literacy field, IMS reporting creates on-going monthly stress through to its restrictions and myriad difficulties with compatibility. More than one problem with IMS exists; the tendencies to only acknowledge employment goals; inaccurate recording of input; loss of input; inability of IMS to self correct; lack of multi-tasking; lack of ability to collate and summarize. Added to this list are the many "patches", fixes that practitioners often only become aware of when they go to input their stats.

ACCOUNTABILITY: LEARNER AND COMMUNITY

More often than not, literacy learners are treated as if they are social outcasts (Weinstein and Lewis 1998), criminals out to beat the system. In the programs, by virtue of social policy, many now have not only a disability to contend with but they are conditioned to embrace defeat and their family responsibilities are not taken seriously (Veeman 2002). It is incomprehensible that the individual is expected to live as if single "like a student" with no heart for the wellbeing of their own children. Otherwise how can a system demand that a family exist on the meager dollars through Ontario works and attend school or job search full time (Ontario Reg. 417/04, OCAP 2004, Hargrave 2004)? As a retired teacher I returned to school after twenty-six years teaching. I found it difficult to manage economically and mentally as a student yet I had the advantage of a long career and a husband working. My children were grown up. Literacy students often have families to support. I didn't have a learning disability. Literacy students often do. I had transportation. Due to financial constraints literacy students do not. Sincere empathy and support for the learner is about ignoring policy that denies responsibility to the learner.

LITERACY TRAINING AND EMPLOYMENT

When the guidelines require that the learner is out of school it includes high-school and Independent Learning Center (ILC) students. ILC provides correspondence courses for high-school credits. Experience indicates that these learners are already motivated individuals who could achieve success if they could access tutoring support in critical reading, writing skills and self-management and self-development skills. It is the literacy practitioners' experiences that more employment and further education goal success can be achieved by including these individuals in the contact hours. However, guidelines do not permit it. LBS programs are in the business of rebuilding an individual's faith in their ability to learn. Employment training belongs to another department. Most literacy learners cannot meet an employment goal in literacy.

CONCLUSION

It is unfortunate that literacy focuses so intently on employment. For many learners the first step is regaining self-worth and confidence. Given the time and opportunity to build self-awareness and develop self most individuals do not entertain the thought of going on to further education. Some learners pushed into literacy through the OW office succeed in making changes but it takes special workers, individualized programming time and patience to make this happen putting a bigger burden on an already overworked practitioner. Sounds like a repeat of Special Ed in the education system. Indeed, this is often where the stigma of literacy has come from – "literacy programs can be considered remedial programs for adults" (Veeman 2002).

"Literacy is about more than reading and writing – it is about how we communicate in society. It is about social practices and relationships, about knowledge, language and culture. Literacy – the use of written communication – finds its place in our lives alongside other ways of communicating. Indeed literacy itself takes many forms: on paper, on the computer screen, on TV, on posters and signs. Those who use literacy take it for granted – but those who cannot use it are excluded from much communication in today's world. Indeed, it is the excluded who can best appreciate the notion of 'literacy as freedom' (UNESCO: 2003). Reading the words, this definition is about the printed word. Reading into the words it is about much more. Social practices, knowledge, language and culture do not depend exclusively on the printed word. Nor do they depend exclusively on employment.

Literacy may mean very different things to the learner than to policy makers who theoretically create policy that represents the needs of the public. A massive population, 42% of the Canadian population (IALS), will not only be trained for but forced to accept low-paying jobs that maintain the status quo of the rich getting richer and poor staying poor. Practitioners will continue to conform to government definitions of employability and literacy and they will be the tools by which government maintains control of a capitalist, patriarchal and hierarchal society. Or, they will give up literacy. Manifest destiny and white privilege appear to have turned inward and the attitude of superiority has only the environment left to destroy.

Within this colonizing system the first inhabitants of North America may have reached the proverbial bottom and many are decolonizing and renewing their original values. Native literacy may indeed be the leader in renewal of self-awareness and self-concept. Given freedom, Native literacy could be the catalyst to peace and contentment with the present instead of the constant improvement of the future that drives society today and that is taking a profound toll on humanity in terms of values, attitudes, stress and spirituality. Accountability in Ontario literacy denies this.

The Canadian Education Association asserts "literacy is both an individual and a social benefit, affecting economic, educational, social and health outcomes for individuals and for society as a whole" (CEA 2004). It appears to veer from Ministry of Training, Colleges and Universities' purely economic/ employment/ fiscal accountability presentation of literacy. Perhaps this discrepancy can explain why in 2004 "almost half of all Canadians function at literacy levels that make it difficult for them to meet their own needs." (CEA 2004) While the CEA definition is closer to wholistic, it still only ministers to the social, intellectual and physical self. Spiritual self continues to be denied.

"Talk about life-long learning has little meaning if [practitioners] are not expected to be life-long learners themselves." (Darville 1992) Dollars are needed to access training that is self chosen and non-prescripted to allow for quality of service to the literacy learner. "Means must be found to resist self-defeating stinginess in program

38

support." (Darville1992)   Many of the learners in fact sabotage their own learning fearing successful completion of their program for it means they must move into the unknown. Practitioners are fully aware that given more time for life-skills training and less on employment skills learners could surmount this barrier.

Wholistic literacy training does not exist in Ontario literacy and the persistent single-mindedness on accountability through employability will continue to prevent it.

CHAPTER 3
ONTARIO NATIVE LITERACY:
A COLONIAL REALITY

Native literacy in Ontario is comprised of twenty-six Literacy and Basic Skills (LBS) programs - a combination of urban in an Aboriginal organization, urban stand-alone and on reserve in a community center. All programs are funded by the Ministry of Training, Colleges and Universities (MTCU) and fully controlled by Literacy and Basic Skills guidelines. Native literacy is a misleading term. It merely provides Ontario government with the appearance of specialization to meet the needs of a cultural group. In actuality Native literacy is required to enforce mainstream thought and value system on Native peoples (Chrisjohn et al 1997:272). Ontario Native literacy, as a cultural stream under Ontario Literacy, must abide by the same policies and procedures as the Anglophone, Francophone and Deaf (G.O.L.D.) streams.

Misguided community expectations that Native literacy will address the unique needs of the Native community, continue to undermine community support of literacy programs. Community interpretation of Native literacy is more about capacity building through Native language and cultural teachings (Assembly of First Nations 1994: iii, 9). Therefore, when literacy programs are required to enforce policies like Workforce/ Workplace Literacy (Belfiore 2002, Sussman 2003, Folinsbee 2001) the possibilities of literacy being part of capacity building and a way to compensate for substandard Native education, get buried in the backlash.

Layers of Native community authority, politics, and attitudes founded in oppression (Adams 1999; Chrisjohn 1997:272), disguise the reality that there is nothing intrinsically Native about Native literacy. Under MTCU outcomes Native literacy is prescripted and controlled by a philosophy of getting people off welfare/Ontario Works (OW), is meant to lead to employability skills for low paying jobs (Workforce/Workplace Literacy OLC 2003; Adams 1990:149), is profoundly under-funded and is unresponsive to its "teachers".

LITERACY AND BASIC SKILLS PROGRAM (LBS) APPLIED TO NATIVE LITERACY

LIFE-LONG LEARNING

The removal of wholistic socialization over the centuries left a void in the Native individual psyche that has long since been filled with dependency (Chrisjohn, Young, Maraun 1997:261-267, Maracle 1996:37). Furthermore, the resultant, purely academic "education" has created more illiteracy in the Native community than it has educated people to prosperity (Antone, Gamlin, Provost-Turchetti 2003; Barman, Hebert, McCaskill 1994:5; Adams 1999: 143; Coalition for the Advancement of Aboriginal Studies (CAAS) 2002:14).

The intent of original, Aboriginal socialization was always to prepare the individual to meet his/her own needs in concert with community needs. Education began before birth and ended at death. In other words the individual learned from birth that potential and/ or gifts would be acknowledged and strengthened for personal as well as community strength throughout a lifetime. Using current vernacular, this can be seen to be "capacity building" or life-long learning.

In 2004, employability skills have been emphasized in literacy. Within these skills, there is a connotation of life skills. Until now, academic skills remained prominent while spirit and emotional development have been denied in the field of literacy. It is interesting how the initial steps in Maslow's Hierarchy of Needs continue to be interpreted as physical needs only, despite "wholistic" being based on Maslow's hierarchy of needs in the literature. Training dollars for transportation and some childcare are available, yet the spirit and emotional needs of individuals burdened by a negative experience in education are not perceived as relevant. Native literacy learners do not need history to repeat itself. In my experience working with Aboriginal adults in the Native Classroom Assistant Diploma Program at Nipissing University and in literacy, I have noted that many individuals who arrive at literacy bring a history of abuse in the education system. Often the physical and emotional abuse by educators is in response to unidentified and/or unaccepted learning difficulties in the children.

QUALITY SERVICE

The Anglophone stream in actuality steers the entire vehicle of literacy by virtue of voice based in numbers. The recent Workforce/ Workplace Train Ontario Initiative is an excellent example. The Anglophone stream created it, piloted it and trained practitioners. The other "cultural" streams had to adapt it to their needs immediately and train the practitioners in their stream within months. Despite several meetings and statements disputing this inappropriate process, in particular for the Native stream, which mostly operates in a Native community with extreme unemployment issues, MTCU pushed ahead and the Native stream found itself doing full day training on using authentic materials to meet the employability goals of their learners. English domination of language and society continues unabated.

Policies based on metropolitan communities cannot meet the needs of the Aboriginal community. Susan Sussman (2003) in *Moving the Markers* explains how statistics from the International Adult Literacy Survey (IALS) and others like it steer policy. Mary Hamilton is quoted in Literacies fall 2003; "IALS operated as a psychometric measurement. It used an information processing model of literacy and attempted to identify levels of literacy skill that are independent of the context of use" (Hamilton 2001). "Test items covered commercial, financial, media, advertising and entertainment related texts; work-place, including job-seeking; consumer manuals and instructions; transportation – related and a recipe" (Hamilton 2001). Aboriginal peoples were not included and considering that "literature (novels, drama, or poetry), autobiography, humour and satire" (Hamilton 2001) were excluded they would have scored low anyway since those are generally the preferred reading for a population who is mostly unemployed.

Additionally, within Sussman's analysis (2003) of IALS is a clear statement that policy fails to take into account the realities of the Aboriginal population. IALS stated that Aboriginal people were not included in the survey because the Aboriginal, immigrant and incarcerated population combined, comprised only 2% of the Canadian population! In other words, taking into consideration research reports and statistics on Aboriginal justice and the penal system which cite illiteracy as extremely relevant, Aboriginal needs are not addressed in any of these literacy policies (Long and Dickason 2000, Movement for Canadian Literacy 2002).

LEARNER CENTERED FOR LEARNERS MOST IN NEED

I have witnessed the freedom that validation of former, negative experiences in educational institutions gives literacy learners. The internalized labels of "retard", "slow learner", "stubborn" and "non-compliant" really do exist and have a profound effect on individual learning. As a teacher and principal in reserve schools for twenty-six years, I grew to abhor the labeling of children and it is one of the reasons I left the profession. Individuals currently label children with disabilities at the time they enter daycare unknowledgeable in: child development; audio-logical processing; speech and language development; learning processes; physical disabilities. As principal of a primary school and as a primary teacher I was often warned about "behaviour problems" due to enter my class or school. The reputation of a four, five or six year old preceded his/her entry and set the stage for years of negative treatment. This results in a child being labeled and often doomed before he/she even gets into the education system. These are some of the adult learners I have been meeting since I entered the field of literacy in 2000.

My frustration with current Native literacy comes from meeting those individuals whom I met in education; who were "Special Ed." (Roeher Institute 1999:1; Cockell and Penney 2001) because they had learning difficulties or were labeled behaviour problems when the system failed to meet their needs; who are now my self identified adult students in North Bay and my learners in literacy. The learners I meet everyday are the "end result" of a system that has become so impersonal through its denial of wholistic worldview that it cannot meet the increasing personal needs it creates in society (Cockell and Penny 2001:39).

Learner-centered means to me that we accept the learner and begin to meet his/her specific needs at that time. The needs of young Aboriginal adults continue to include awareness and general knowledge about the constraints of the reserve world they have left and the world they are attempting to enlist in. The education system generally offered at the reserve level has consistently disregarded Aboriginal culture and history. Young people now suffer from a forced ignorance of the influences on their lives. They are unaware of the degree of control Indian Affairs has over their health, education, living standard and identity. Through the Indian Act their ethnicity, land ownership, burial, marital rights, birthright and place called home are in constant state of uncertainty (Monture-Angus 1999; McNab 1999; Miller 2004). The implicit right to dominate, to be first, most qualified and most suitable "white privilege" will continue to exert its power no matter where they are in the western world or what they accomplish (Kendall 2001). Systemic racism founded in stereotypes and unconsciously imbedded in policies, legislation will continually test their determination (Bell 2004:29-30). "Ethnostress" describes the conditions and results that years of oppressive experience have had on Aboriginal people. Identified in *Aboriginal Access to Post-Secondary Education* (Hill 1995) it plays a significant role in the defeat of fragile visions of young Aboriginal people.

ACCOUNTABILITY: POLITICAL

The Ontario Native Literacy Coalition (ONLC) a voluntary, non-profit, provincial network that represents the twenty-six Native community Literacy and Basic Skills (LBS) programs was incorporated in 1988 to assist with Ministry of Training Colleges and Universities (MTCU). In reality ONLC gets full funding from MTCU and is mandated to enforce policies of MTCU, a little recognized fact that has come out of this research. For this Aboriginal academic it raises concerns regarding my continued involvement with ONLC. Would Howard Adams (1999), B.A. Sociology, PhD History, retired Métis educator and activist, describe me as "Aboriginal bourgeoisie" or would I be considered one of the "leaders who promote non-indigenous goals and embody non- indigenous values and who is used by the state to maintain its control" (Alfred 1999: xiv).

Funding agreements are often signed by a third party administrator or executive Director, so that the Native literacy practitioner has not read, interpreted or had input into it. This has come to light in the past year at two Native literacy gatherings (North Bay 05/04, AGM Burleigh Falls 10/04). These agreements exact specific services and loyalty, with more emphasis on satisfying government policy than on the learner; agreements lacking the flexibility to address the diversity of Native Peoples' needs and barriers (MTCU 2000). Literal interpretation of the agreement demands absolute adherence to issues that alienate Native literacy. These include 1) all materials created with MTCU funds are the property of MTCU including enduring copyright which results in programs reluctant to share their expertise verbally or in writing, 2) programs founded in life skills, crafts, or Native languages have been shut down causing others to hide their strengths. 3) age barriers that deny child and youth access thus insisting on intervention instead of prevention and 4) persistent priority of employability skills defeats the concept of capacity building in Native communities, where self development needs to come first (Friere 2000 a): 47, 114, 174-175).

ACCOUNTABILITY: LEARNER AND COMMUNITY

Illiteracy accounts for high unemployment and escalating numbers living in poverty on reserves and on urban streets. Illiteracy will imprison them there (Farrell, Aubry, and Reissing 2002). Owing to the dysfunction in the communities (Boldt 1993:176, Adams 1999:3, Bird, Land, Macadam 2002: 92-108, Friere 2000 a):152) and the extreme lack of economic growth, employment skills are not seen as the first need of Native learners.

Due to minimal funding, programs are dependent in so many ways, that they cannot stand tall as a community leader in capacity building. They have no cash flow: for promotion; to hire sufficient staff to meet the individual needs of learners as they arrive; to access sufficient space and time for programming; to purchase appropriate Aboriginal resources for the learners; to purchase needed equipment to operate an adult education program; to purchase a library that would attract learners and promote literacy.

There are many documents written recording the needs of Aboriginal individuals and communities. Most express the vision of "change[ing] the dismal literacy situation for our people, provide[ing] full opportunities for personal growth and development, eliminate[ing] our poverty and dependency and fulfill[ing] the dreams of our ancestors to rebuild our First Nations into self-reliant people, to be in the same teepee, nurturing the same fire and communicating in the equality of the circle in order to meet community needs." (Assembly of First Nations 1994: iii)

Practitioners see self-awareness and development that have been denied throughout history as needed literacy training for Native learners (Hampton in Battiste1995; Cockell and Penney 2001:39; George 1998; Logan and McClain 2003; Brant and George 1997). They are in agreement with Menno Boldt (1993) "Unless [Native people] can revitalize their traditional philosophies and principles they will become extinct as "Indians"; that they will survive only as a legal-racial category defined in the Indian Act" (Boldt 1993: xvi).

Literacy training needs to be available to all ages in the Aboriginal community. Children modeling parents, has been disturbed since the residential school era. Residential schools deprived communities of parental rights and responsibilities to the point that school personnel, church and governments, have become more the model than parents. In the Aboriginal communities, isolated as they are, this left a vacuum that has since been filled with dysfunction affected by a disconnection between instinct and reality. With no models and an education system that has generally maintained the attitude that the average Aboriginal child is incapable and unlovable, Aboriginal communities have long suffered the influence of a very narrow, negative vision of the future. And, even though in recent years the inter-generational impact of the residential school era has been acknowledged and the specifics documented (Chrisjohn 1997, Grant 1996, Bussidor and Bilgen-Reinart 1997, Knockwood 1992) in terms of the psychological and emotional impacts that continue to be passed on as legacy there is no accommodation and this author believes the abuse goes on. In this context then, literacy is a family reality.

LITERACY TRAINING AND EMPLOYMENT

Meeting the challenge of a 64% unemployed, Aboriginal population in Ontario requires creative solutions (George 1998:8) and policy based on statistics becomes the enemy in Aboriginal literacy. Susan Sussman (2003) clarifies that statistics are used to create policy, a move that clearly supports this claim.

One set of factors affecting Native employment and identified by Kuhn and Sweetman (2004) relate to the conflict the Native literacy field has regarding Workforce/ Workplace Literacy: "unlike immigrants, [Aboriginal peoples] are not a self-selected group who voluntarily chose to migrate in search of greater economic opportunity". A former prosperous society has been forced into a situation of poverty in their assigned, unproductive portions of their own land (Adams 1999:7). Practitioners see the low-paying-job readiness as a defeatist approach (OLC 2003).

While MTCU holds fast to the definition of literacy as an upgrading tool the federal government through HRDC (2005) sees it as "skills to participate in modern society, whether it is to read a bus schedule or the daily newspaper, to calculate the dosage for medication, to use a computer program, or to follow and engage in a debate about government policy". The HRSDC statement goes on to say that, "Low literacy skills can be a barrier to having the highly skilled productive work force and strong thriving communities that underpin a high standard of living"(Government of Canada 2003:1). Unfortunately, despite its application to all segments of Canadian society this statement appears to apply only to urban, metropolitan society not to rural Canada. Several policies require exposure to an abundance of low paying jobs and dependence on a surplus of volunteers, neither of which are to be found in Aboriginal communities.

Native communities exist in minute, isolated, economically destitute portions of a country they once traveled freely. Despite evidence that Canada is not to be blessed with George Catlin (1796-1872) and Edward Curtis' (1868-1952) "vanishing Indians" as presented at *Wooden Indians & Stereotypical Imagery*; that in fact the Aboriginal population growth is surpassing that of the dominant society; government personnel and policy insists on ignoring the reality. Russel Barsh (1994) acknowledges this phenomenon in his 1994 article *"Social Integration or Disintegration?"* Haddad and Spivey (1992) go further and state that an "alliance between the federal government and the business sector, keeps Native communities in a state of dependency". Haddad and Spivey go on to say that "The dominant group, in effect, is able to sustain the underdeveloped state of Native [people of Canada] by controlling the Native [peoples'] access to capital, technology, and other resources necessary." Communities contend with a constant struggle for employment through grant opportunities which create fierce competition for few dollars which in turn creates territorial battles (Adams 1999:123-148; Boldt 1994: xvi; Monture-Angus 1999:11; Alfred 1999:27) - battles that disguise the possibility that when the education system refuses to support socialization into the wholistic Native world view, Native literacy could at the very least be an intervention (CAAS 2002, Bell 2004, Gaikezheyongai 2000).

The *Royal Commission on Aboriginal Peoples* (RCAP 1993) clearly identified reality in Native communities almost ten years ago. "Aboriginal people endure ill health, run-down and overcrowded housing, polluted water, inadequate schools, poverty and family breakdown at rates found more often in developing countries than in Canada. These conditions are inherently unjust. They put the future of Aboriginal communities in peril". (Minister Supply and Services Canada 1996 3:59) It would appear that the Ontario government pays no heed to the RCAP findings as Native literacy practitioners have been advocating for a more relevant literacy program to no avail (Rodriquez and Sawyer 1990, Saskatchewan Indian Institute of Technologies 1990, Ontario MET 1993, Assembly of First Nations 1994, Hill 1995, Brant and George 1997, ONLC 1998, Thompson 2002, Lepine 2003, Logan and McClain 2003). A plan may be to carry the RCAP Report to MTCU/Umbrella meetings.

Further it would seem that although provincial government derives much of its funding from federal government there is no recognition that the federal government has a fiduciary responsibility for the education of Aboriginal people of Canada (Monture-Angus 1999) and that literacy has been put in the position of righting past education wrongs (Longfield 2003, Assembly of First Nations 1988).

RECOGNIZING THE NEED TO DECOLONIZE

"In Canada, as elsewhere much of Native writing, whether blunt or subtle, is protest literature in that it speaks to the process of our colonization: dispossession, objectification, marginalization, and that constant struggle for cultural survival expressed in the movement for structural and psychological self-determination"(Armstrong 1993). Ontario literacy continues the colonization that created current reality in the Native community and by using the term Native literacy, people - Aboriginal people in particular - are led to believe that the impact of that colonization is being dealt with.

"Many Aboriginal people will need to undergo a process of self-examination to uncover the cultural assumptions that they have internalized from Western culture. This is important as many of these internalized assumptions invalidate traditional Aboriginal beliefs and practices." (Hill 1999:66) This need is apparent to practitioners in Native literacy. (Gaikezheyongai 2000, Logan and McClain 2003, Lepine 2003, George 1998) "If we realize that these destructive feelings and behaviour are only patterns of distress, then we can move to rid ourselves of them. We can learn to heal our-selves and move towards our personal and collective liberation..." (Hill 1999: 67) Bob Mullaly, Professor of Social Work, explains why policy that prevents this growth is so strong. "Oppression is perpetrated by dominant groups and is systemic and continuous in its application. Oppression protects a kind of citizenship that is [allegedly] superior to that of the oppressed. Oppression carries out certain social functions for the dominant group by ensuring that society reproduces itself and maintains the same dominant-subordinate relationships" (Mullaly 1997:138-9).

NATIVE LITERACY MUST BE UNIQUE

To meet the challenges Native literacy is and must be different. Native community and individual needs are different and so must the methodology and guidelines that meet them (Bossort, Monnastes and Malnarich 2000:58).

Employment as a success standard (Hampton 1998:21, Maracle1996:4) has once again been foisted on the Native community through the Workforce /Workplace Literacy Initiative (OLC 2003), finalized in 2004 by Ministry of Training, Colleges and Universities (MTCU). While Workforce/ Workplace Literacy currently demoralizes stakeholders in Native literacy this same standard of success has been referenced many times in the literature as one of the faults that has defeated and continues to defeat the Native education progress (Milloy 1999, Bird, Land, Macadam 2002, Barman, Hebert, McCaskill 1994, Hart 2002, Chrisjohn et al 1997).

The situation that Jane E. Henson (1982) describes in *Pedagogy and Politics in Native Literacy Projects: the Case of the Native Adult Learning Group*, speaks directly to the issue of attending to the impact of Canadian Aboriginal history as a necessary component of Native literacy. Henson prefaces her work; "It is a fundamental assumption of this article that Native illiteracy both results from and in turn contributes to the colonial relations characteristic of Native-dominant society interactions in all spheres." Howard Adams (1999) comprehensively describes the on-going repercussions of colonialism in the Aboriginal community. In *Tortured People* he describes how "Aboriginal bourgeoisie" now enforce their own version of colonialism. Works of both Howard Adams (1999) and Barbara – Helen Hill (2002), author of *Shaking the Rattle: a Guide to*

Healing the Wounds of Colonization, do much to explain the need to change the intent of Native literacy.

Literacy can no longer be accepted as just reading, writing and numeracy. Without identity, wellness, awareness of "white privilege" and general knowledge of mainstream society the Aboriginal individual lacks the requirements to thrive outside of the Aboriginal community. This is abundantly clear when the works of Aboriginal professors, academics, psychologists, therapists, social workers and educators in literacy are analyzed. (See chapter 4)

Reading through recent MTCU literacy policies (Grieves 2005), frequent mention is made of "self-management and self-direction" in terms of "essential skills". Admittedly the connotation of these terms is dependent on the reader's experiential perception, however if the goal of literacy is to empower the individual such that he/she becomes employable, identity, wellness and knowledge of many, many schema are to be considered essential.

Emile Durkheim (Ashley and Orenstein 1990: 121) famous French sociologist described the phenomenon of dysfunction that afflicts the Aboriginal population. Anomie, "an absence, confusion, or conflict in the norms of [Aboriginal] society becomes a psychological state of disorder and meaninglessness" (Marshall 1998:21). Although Durkheim was describing a shift in society based on economics in response to industrialization in Europe, the similarities with post contact, Canadian Aboriginal society, is unmistakable. In *Shaking the Rattle: a Guide to Healing the Wounds of Colonization*, Barbara-Helen Hill (2002) quotes Diane Hill's *The Power within People* (Hill 1985); "Anomie denotes a people's loss of faith and belief in their institutions, values, and existence." Barbara-Helen Hill adds to the contributions of Howard Adams, Jane-Middleton-Moz (1989:174) and Jenny Horsman (1999:169-210) in terms of barriers that must be surmounted to allow the Aboriginal literacy learner to learn. Clarification of the depth of damage and omnipresent need for righting the effects of "Canadian" history in Aboriginal society is the constant theme in journal articles, research reports, conference reports and books on the topic of Native literacy training (CRRF 2002; Horsman 2004; Aboriginal Healing and Wellness 2000;

Lepine 2003; Logan-Elliott and McClain 2003; Antone, Gamlin and Provost-Turchetti (2003); RCAP 1993; Henson 1982; Jackson, McCaskill, Hall 1982; Cockell and Penney 2001; Etkin 1991; Haddad and Spivey 1992; Barsh 1994; Bossort, Monnastes and Malnarich 1990).

Sociologists, Karl Marx and Friederich Engles predicted the proletarianization of society "the process by which sections of the middle class becomes absorbed into the working class" (Marshall 1998:530). Government control of all levels of education including literacy would appear to create the process to accomplish modern day version of this process. Workers at every level of the education spectrum, daycare to post-secondary, are fully controlled by the platform of Canadian government. For this author, it explains the dogged MTCU Consultants' support of a literacy system that supports government and fails the learner.

Karl Marx described how labour and management would be separated from ownership of capital and thus the labour force dehumanized (Marshall 1998:530); perhaps this explains the myriad levels of governing bodies – expanding numbers of managers, administrators and professionals whom government insists on 'licensing' and who are so far removed from grassroots they don't understand the impact of what they enforce. Aboriginal lawyer Patricia Montour-Angus and Aboriginal professor and Consultant Janice Acoose describe this insistence on certification and licensing in the Aboriginal community as violence – violating human rights and recognition of achievement. Chrisjohn et al describe qualifications/ certification as "primarily political processes used to marginalize those who ask too many embarrassing questions and identify those who "bought in" and so are acceptable to the mainstream." (Chrisjohn et al 1997:295)

Aboriginal people have long experienced the violence and control of government education. Staggering dropout rates show little improvement over a thirty-year period as illustrated by the following statistics. The "Hawthorn Report of 1967 reports a 94% dropout rate. By 1988 the National Review Report of 80% shows an increase and the Canada West Foundation 2003 report at 75%" indicates very little improvement. (Bell 2004).

Jenny Horsman explains the impact of that trauma on learning. Horsman who has been "exploring how violence affects learning" wrote an eighty-three page research report which describes how "responses to trauma support or limit learning possibilities"(Horsman 2004:1) In as much as Horsman's research is about high-school youth it serves to endorse the concept that Native literacy is operating at the wrong end of the learning continuum a position created by the fact that the foundation of Native literacy is not wholistic.

Horsman is particularly expressive about society coming to understand that abuse does not make an individual abnormal. Abuse creates barriers. It is these barriers that are described by Aboriginal writers – academics, historians, poets, novelists, and educators – many revealing reality in their traditional storytelling mode.

Much of Horsman's research supports this paper's claim that until Native literacy follows its own path, the status quo of the Aboriginal population, with or without self-government, will not change because current literacy perpetuates capitalism based on skilled labour and exploitation of resources, neither of which Canada has granted the Aboriginal population. Genuine "Native" literacy cannot happen until the Aboriginal concept of wholistic is applied to literacy training. All components, functions, generations, cycles, responsibilities and relationships of being involved in learners' lives require consideration if the training is to provide empowerment.

The Aboriginal population is in need of righting intergenerational problems of low literacy as well as prevention of the perpetuation of illiteracy (Chrisjohn et al 1997). In this context it is clear that MTCU dictates of literacy for employment are inappropriate for the Native literacy field.

Wholistic literacy training means, "learning to read the world" as Friere and Macedo (1987) wrote – a much more powerful definition. This is related to a worldview that does not fragment mental, physical, spiritual and emotional elements of self nor deny the interconnectedness in creation, as is the case for Aboriginal peoples.

Katrina Grieve's (2003) OLC *Research Project on Self-management and Self-direction* the continuation of Ojibway literacy practitioner Christiana Jones' *Self-Management and Self-Direction in the Success of Native Literacy Learners* (2003) stops short of supporting Aboriginal concept of wholistic literacy. Despite the inclusion of mental, physical, social and emotional self as per Jones, Grieves qualifies "bringing the whole self - including spirit, emotions, mind and body to learning" with the statement; "This process may⁵ increase self-awareness and help us find ways to support our own learning". Once more Native philosophy is discounted with one three-letter English word. To the Native literacy worker there is no doubt.

There is no shortage of literature on the need for self-esteem as the first step to learning. Self-esteem however, is contingent on an individual's self-worth, which is contingent on self-concept, which again is contingent on identity. It is this "clear contrast with the kinds of programs and services that exist in mainstream society (AHW: 2000:31) that overwhelms the Native literacy field. Programs that claim to be holistic but which deny the interrelationship of so many aspects of life and being. In dominant society, accreditation, certification and specialization require a human being to attempt to build a positive self-image in so many places, at the hands of so many people, and through so many policies it is no wonder that the individual becomes fragmented (Chrisjohn et al 1997:303).

CONCLUSION

The growing population of homeless, a reality in every Canadian metropolitan area, highlights the looming specter of a two-class Canadian society that harkens to the days of the industrial revolution that Karl Marx, Emile Durkheim and Max Webber analyzed. Karl Marx (Ashley and Orenstein 1990) in particular, described the use of institutions to create a capitalist society. He theorized the false consciousness that would program the working class/poor masses to accept, even claim their own part in creating their situation that

---

5 My own emphasis: the word "may" indicates only possibility, which detracts from the validity of Aboriginal worldview.

allows the acceptance of government and powerful organizations to rule the world.

Despite presentation of homelessness by government and media, as a chosen lifestyle (Toronto Correspondent 2000, Jones 2000; Beavis, Klos, Carter and Douchant 1997) those who work with the homeless know differently. Moreover, Government policy underlies the daily woes of more than half of the Canadian population. Policies guiding Ontario Works (OW), Ontario Disability Support program (ODSP), Unemployment Insurance (UI), and Workman's Compensation fail to provide sufficient, stable resources for the average individual to reinvent his/her self after the economic climate stifles their employment goals and the education's system defeats them from the beginning.

In response to 500 years of oppression many Aboriginal individuals (therefore communities) have internalized the false consciousness of their lack of capability to recognize their own needs and the solutions to meeting those needs. Many communities struggle under the false belief that they are in control of their destiny when in fact it is the Department of Indian Affairs through the Indian Act that is in control.

In addition, community members are for the most part, unaware of the "missing pieces" in their educational experience – life-skills, problem solving, and identity. Another barrier to individual and community acceptance and support of literacy programs, is the "stigma attached" – literacy as special education for adults (Ministry of Education Literacy Branch.1993:73) to literacy training. Aboriginal individuals have learned after centuries of stereotyping, to fend off any indication that they are deficient.

A poignant example of this is the reaction of the Aboriginal community to the findings of Dr. William Scaldwell's (1985) report on the medical condition of Otitis Media - an infection of the inner ear which when chronic creates many forms of hearing impairment. At the time the reports caught my attention because I recalled the numerous times my mother had to nurse one of my brothers through an earache. As well, there were always several children in the school I was teaching in who were victims of chronic earaches. In retrospect, many of these individuals exhibited some degree of atypical behaviour – attention seeking, attention deficit, defiance and non-compliance. Shortly after that I met Dr. Scaldwell when his partner Janet Frame taught in the Native Classroom Assistant Program (NCADP) with me at Nipissing University. Over the summer Dr. Scaldwell shared his research with me. The point that Dr. Scaldwell was making was that it takes more days on antibiotics for the Aboriginal individual to truly get rid of the infection. This can make it chronic for the infection is never really cured; it merely rebuilds allowing more permanent damage. He expressed his regret that the Aboriginal population in general had reacted with anger to his finding that it is a physical formation of the inner ear that causes Aboriginal children and adults to be susceptible to Otitis Media. Imagine the trauma and hearing damage this can cause when a child may have had as many as twelve by school age!

I studied the repercussions of Otitis Media and began sharing materials and strategies for improving audiological processing with my summer adult students. Aboriginal people resist being identified in any way and entering a "literacy" program as they are currently defined by MTCU, would indicate a deficiency especially since government has been promoting the "deficit model" for years (Darville 1992; Friere 1985, 2000; Horsman 1999)

Low literacy skills initiated by Otitis Media are not simply an adult issue in the Aboriginal community. In the last ten years, universities and colleges have been recruited by Indian Affairs to assist with higher education for Aboriginal individuals. Programs have been created to provide university access to Aboriginal people. For many mature students doors have opened. However, the requisite skills for attending post secondary institutions are still not being attended to and these students are being allowed to fail in the university setting. In their own minds they fail the Aboriginal community. In reality the doors for many were never really opened. However, in their ignorance of required academic skills, learners are led to believe that they are solely at fault.

These particular university programs have begun to highlight the literacy needs of not only the mature, diploma students but also recent graduates of high-schools. The number of Aboriginal post-secondary students who graduate with a degree is minimal in comparison with the numbers registered in post secondary institutions. During my years as; a parent of post secondary students; full-time post secondary student; tutor of post secondary students, I have come to see that foundational life skills are missing. Awareness of the social, political, economical and academic requirements of living in the dominant society is insufficient to allow equitable opportunities. Diane Hill, Mohawk healer and educator, author of several articles on Aboriginal education, further clarifies these barriers in *Aboriginal Access to Post-secondary Education* (Hill 1995, 1999). Could this result of 12 years of formal education, be the counterpart to the result of removing children from their parents and community and all exposure to cultural influences? The Royal Commission on Aboriginal Peoples says "yes" (1996:Vol.3:441). Far too many Aboriginal young people do not have the required literacy skills to survive well in either world.

The layers of colonization are imbedded in the layers of literacy needs. The layers include great grandparents with some knowledge of traditional practices and very little understanding of how historical events and legislation rule their lives and misguided expectations of the education system; grandparents with little or no knowledge of traditional practices, some misrepresented knowledge and little understanding of historical events and legislation that control their lives as well as misguided expectations of the education system; parents with a growing knowledge of some stereotypical, traditional practices, little knowledge of historical events that control their lives, insufficient information to evaluate systems of values; young people with no traditional knowledge, poorly fitting colonial, patriarchal values, attempting to live in mainstream with the false consciousness that they can override white privilege with education.

Current literacy training in Ontario does not award the Aboriginal population the capacity building needed at this time in their history. At a time when dominant society through government has condescended to negotiate self-government, Aboriginal communities and organizations require strong identity and skilled leadership. When statistics and Native writers indicate that the education system has failed in this regard a solution must be found elsewhere. Native literacy redefined can be seen to be that source.

CHAPTER 4
WHOLISTIC NATIVE LITERACY

INTRODUCTION

Native worldview embraces healing and prevention rather than intervention (Grant 1996:31- 46, Barman, Hebert, McCaskill 1987:3) but that philosophy appears to hold no place in Native literacy as it currently exists within Ontario literacy. Moreover, based on a comprehensive literature review of literacy, there is no conclusive definition of literacy; hence one could assume that a definition of Native Literacy would not challenge current literacy philosophy.

Documented needs resulting from Native history and education as well as a known "methodology" held in blood memory create the vision of "reclaiming, reconnecting and reordering those ways of knowing, in the process of freeing ourselves. Change must be the basis for education/literacy and cultural development. It begins with learning." (Battiste, Youngblood - Henderson 2000: 9; Maracle 1996: 92; Smith1999: 69) "The organizing and regulating force for group order and endeavor was custom and tradition. Customs were derived from the Creator and because they were spiritually endorsed and through history had withstood the test of time they represented the Creator's blueprint for the survival of the tribe" (Boldt and Long 1985: 543). Nor can "the triad of poverty, powerlessness and anomie" (RCAP 1993:42) that overwhelms Native communities be put right through "ideologies that convince their recipients that their own values and beliefs are no longer valid (RCAP 1993:19)". A methodology in Native literacy is needed that is consistent with Aboriginal knowledge. "The spirit carries with it all of the accumulated knowledge of past and present lives. It includes remembered events from both awake and sleeping states. The dream world, through its ties to the spirituality of the individual is an inherent part of the Native individual's overall psychology" (Gibbs 1988). Paula Gunn Allen Professor of English, University of California, provides a further explanation of "blood memory" as "a solid, impregnable and eradicable orientation toward a spirit- informed view of the universe, which provides an internal structure to our consciousness" (Gunn Allen 1992:165, 168).

Even as there is no conclusive definition of literacy in general (Newman1994:16-25, 28, 37-38, 74), a definition of Native Literacy rooted in original, Native worldview, is feasible. A foundation for a Native perspective on Native literacy is to be found in *Revitalization of Indian Cultural Survival Schools* (McCaskill 1987:153-179 in Barman, et al); *Locally Developed Native Studies Curriculum: an Historical and Philosophical Rationale* (Archibald 1998:288-312 in Battiste and Barman); the Introduction to *Protecting Indigenous Knowledge and Heritage* in (Battiste and Youngblood Henderson 2000:12-13); and *Law Politics and Tradition* (Maracle 1996:41). Native literacy is part of the healing journey as per the Aboriginal Healing and Wellness Strategy (2000:31). Native people need to know the value in their original teachings. They are entitled to the opportunity to rebuild their identity through Native processes and rewriting of their pre and post-contact history. Through understanding the source of the anomie that constrains current Native community Native individuals can regain the personal power that will in turn empower the community.

For these reasons, I define wholistic Native literacy as a continuum of relevant knowledge and guidance that sets in motion the healing of the psychological impact of Native history and that provides individual and community access to skills development that increases self-determination. Imbedded in this definition are the components: social, spiritual, political, and academic literacy as well as relevant pedagogies (Barman et al 1987:165, Fiere1985:14, Barman et al 1994:24-27, Smith 1999:131,132). Marlene Brant Castellano describes the Aboriginal concept of wholistic: "the circle representing the cycle of life, contains all experiences, everything in the biosphere – animal, vegetable, mineral, human, spirit – past, present and future." (Castellano 2000:30)

My career and this paper have been guided by a dedication to provide effective education for the Native individual since 1969. In fact it amazed me in 1994 to find so much literature on Native education that put into print what I had experimented with and found successful[6]. Reflective teaching in adult education from 1983 to 2004 in the Native Classroom Assistant Diploma Program (NCADP) in North Bay, has not only given me insight into the needs in Native communities across Ontario, it also gives me the opportunity to pilot wholistic strategies through my students.

While a degree in Native Studies provides me with curriculum, studies in psychology and Native Education explain why the inclusion of Native content and methods has such a profound, positive influence on the students. It explains also why so many Aboriginal community members are so adamantly opposed to things "Native" (Friere1985: 16, Maracle 1996:110, Adams 1999 123-136).

In their discussion with the Tlinget and Haida, Nora Marks Dauenhauer and Richard Dauenhauer realized a concept of "mid-generation" (now 51-81years of age) that describes the reality that there is a significant group of Native people in the community that "embraces political correctness – neo-positivism" (Dauenhauer and Dauenhauer 1999:27-33). These are the individuals who believed it best to "ignore" traditional practices and accept eurocentrism in the belief that their children would escape the violence and fare better in dominant society. Their offspring "in what George Tinker (Tinker 1993 in Irwin 2000: 24) calls the praxis of self-hatred [became] convinced that 'Indian' truly is evil, savage, heathen, and that any 'Indian' ways are the devil's work".

Howard Adams' (1999) explanation of the dysfunction in the Native community reinforced the understanding I acquired through study in organizational psychology and management skills. Resistance

---

6 In 1994 a career move to Peterborough ON offered me my first opportunity to take university courses on campus at Trent University. Prior to that, I had taken them through correspondence.

to Native literacy as a continuation of colonization and Eurocentric education is common practice in the communities now.

Courses in my master's degree in Sociology and Equity Studies in Education at OISE/UT have contributed to my understanding of conscious and unconscious influences in the Native community. Studies in sociology have directed me to the sources of continuing unsuccessful education of Native children and the reason Native literacy cannot gain ground in its mission to alleviate the illiteracy that maintains the status quo for Native people in Canada. Colonialism (Smith 1999), imperialism (Smith 1999, Adams 1999), false-consciousness (Marx in Ashley and Orenstein 1993), Aboriginal bourgeoisie (Adams 1999), plastic elders (Resolution of the 5th Annual Meeting of the Traditional Elder's Conference 1980), and many more concepts learned through Aboriginal scholars, writers and academics clarify my experiences in the education field thus far. It has solidified my knowledge that healing in the Native community will happen only when we realize that it is the education system that is a mechanism of oppression and we must likewise begin to avert it (Friere1985:167-17, Adams 1999:8, Monture-Angus 1999:158, Maracle 1996:90). Within Eber Hampton's *Redefinition of Indian Education* are many explanations of "a school system as the enemy" but more important are Hampton's insights into creating "an education worthy of [us] and our ancestors" (Hampton 1995). Native literacy can begin that process; can clarify the oppression and begin the journey of healing (Gaikezheyongai 2000, 23, 25, George 1993:7-15, Native Literacy Research Report 1993:63).

Relative to Native literacy: first, there is no such thing as "Native" literacy. It is a name only; a third component of the cultural streams in Ontario literacy, the others being the Francophone and the G.O.L.D (deaf). Second, all programs and networks sign an identical, generic funding agreement[7] with Ministry of Training Colleges and Universities (MTCU); with extreme restrictions on programming and administration; that allows for no differentiation in Native literacy.

---

7 ONLC and program agreements were studied and compared by the ONLC president.

Literacy training identified as one hope for the Native unemployed is restricted through lack of definition and by government policy that not only caters to the more fortunate but creates economic and social barriers for the less fortunate (Hargrave 2004, Hampton 1995:34, Newman 1994:16-25, Adams 1999:147, Hill 1995:53). While "many personal, situational and institutional barriers" (Hill 1995:53) are shared with all adult learners, the unique cultural background of Aboriginal adult learners adds more (Hill 1999:87). The funding for literacy in Canada comes from the education "pot" exacting promise not to criticize formal education institutions (Chall in Venezky, Wagner, Ciliberte 1990:56) hence prevention of illiteracy is out of reach. Literacy has become a branch of the education ministry. Education is expected to provide literacy. Emphasis on employability confounds efforts at wholistic Native literacy as it continues to leave out spiritual, emotional and physical elements of life while refusing to address historical psychological damage. "The identity of [Native] people is that which links our history and our future to this day."(Battiste and Barman 1998:22) Current Native literacy needs to address the false identity that the Native learner has adopted as a result of history, stereotyping and misrepresentation (Smith 1999:23).

A small body of research in Native Literacy, found on the Adult Literacy Data Base (NALD) maintains it should be different not only from Ontario literacy but it also cannot repeat the formal education experience of most Aboriginal learners. Additionally, Native literacy needs to be wholistic to address needs of the spirit, heart, mind and body, created by the past and present (Gaikezheyongai 2000, Cockell and Penny 2001, Native Literacy Research Report 1993, George 1993) but there is very little that defines and distinguishes a methodology.

A definition of Native literacy can be determined by reflexive research that is based on my personal experience as an educator, student, grandmother, and mother and my research in Sociology and Equity Studies in Education and Native Studies. I will support my definition of Native Literacy by use of reflexive research methodology (Arvay 1998, Munby and Russell 1994, Cunliff 2003). The reasoning;

typical research methodology is inappropriate and in fact defeating in this context. This is clarified by Eber Hampton, President of the Saskatchewan Indian Federated University in his article "First Nations Controlled University Education" in Castellano et al 2000: 214. Adams 1999:8-12 and Ristock and Pennell1996:1-15, 43, 49 argue it and Smith in "Colonizing Knowledges" (1999:68-72) states that "Third world intellectuals have to position themselves strategically as intellectuals within the academy. 'I will speak for myself as a Third World person' is an important position for political mobilization today." Smith states, "But the real demand is that, when I speak from that position, I should be listened to seriously; not with…benevolent imperialism." Further, I use the term Native in response to the title, Native Literacy.

I will use my experiences in the Native community as a status member and educator from 1969 to 2004 to support the development of my understanding of socialization, education and literacy training as one and the same. Additionally, I will use my literature review to validate the findings I have accumulated during those thirty-five years. This merging of experience and research results in a definition of wholistic Native literacy (Antone, Gamlin and Provost-Turchetti 2003, Gaikezheyongai 2000) that could birth a new era for those Native people who have been failed by education and society. References to these failures have been documented in the literature: Hampton's "Towards a Redefinition of Indian Education" in Battiste and Barman 1998: 6-19; Marie Battiste's article "Micmac Literacy and Cognitive Assimilation" in Barman et al 1999: 23-41, and Monture-Angus 1999:158-163 in her chapter "Closing the Circle".

NATIVE WHOLISTIC LITERACY AND PEDAGOGY

"Everything is related by virtue of shared origins. The human being is an entire whole mentally, physically, spiritually, and emotionally, as an individual with one's family and extended family, one's people and with the cosmos in sacred relationships".
(Antone, Gamlin, Provost-Turchetti 2003)

Within Native wholistic worldview and pedagogy there are four stages of life, four cycles of human development, four dimensions of true learning, four cardinal directions, four grandfathers, four elements of the physical world, four aspects to our nature, four winds, four elements to our identity. Everything involves four: stages; cycles; times; aspects; elements. Such things as life, time, plant/animal kingdom, and cycles function in terms of four.

Original socialization adhered to the concept of interconnectedness in all ways. Interconnectedness attached gifts and responsibilities to every part of creation. Native concept of wholistic: four stages of life – childhood, adolescence, adulthood, elders; four seasons; four quarters of the life-cycle – 0-25 learning, 25-50 employment, 50 -75 preparation for retirement, 75-100 retirement and Elderhood; four times of the day; four elements of creation; four aspects of self - physical, emotional, spiritual, intellectual; four aspects of identity-body awareness, self-concept, self-esteem, self-determination; four symbolic races of man, allowed for equality based in spirituality.

In addition, the interconnectedness of past, present and future inspired circumspection in each word and action. "If people find no room in their lives to pray or meditate, to reflect deeply on why they have been created, and what they must do with their lives, and listen with all their being to the guidance of the universe, then those people are like birds who have not yet learned to fly. All parts of the bird are present, but something is missing. To be a whole person is to be alive in a physical, emotional, mental and spiritual way" (Lane, Bopp, Bopp, and Brown 1985:56).

Paulo Friere, Brazilian educator and literacy activist describes wholistic in the Native sense many times in his writings on empowerment (Friere 2000 a). In fact, it was energizing when I read his works and realized that during my thirty-four years in Native education I have been an "agent of change". Further, using my concept of education as the continuation of empowering socialization was Friere's concept of literacy training (Friere 1985).

Education, socialization and literacy are not separate foci in the Native world but are one and the same and include the four divisions of the life cycle; all school age levels; elementary, secondary, postsecondary. It is this interrelatedness that instructs Native literacy to be different from Ontario literacy and wholistic if it is to assist learners who for a variety of reasons failed in the education system. The age of the learner matters not for "the intellectual, physical and spiritual aspects of the [learner] must be viewed wholistically without the separation between secular and sacred knowledge which characterizes schooling in the dominant Canadian society" (Barman et al 1994:5).

HEALING IN THE MEDICINE WHEEL APPROACH

I believe that while many Native authors and researchers articulated philosophy of Native learning and teaching I was "piloting" it. I believe this to be true because I didn't get the opportunity to take Native Studies courses until 1975 when I began taking one per year by correspondence. By the time I studied Native education and spirituality I was at the end of my elementary teaching career in 2000. Reflective teaching during twenty-six years as an elementary school teacher in Native communities (1969 to 2000) modified my curriculum to include Native Studies and methodology based in Medicine Wheel teachings of responsibility, equality and spirituality (Lane, Bopp, Bopp and Brown 2003, Beck, Walters and Francisco 1992, Hart 2002, Graveline 1998, Battiste and Barman 1998). The core of the curriculum was; self-awareness, responsibility, spirituality and respect. Eber Hampton's reflections on Native education in Battiste and Barman (1998:5-46) reflected these same principles.

My intent to "teach children in a manner that enhances consciousness of being an Indian and a fully participating citizen of Canada" (Battiste and Barman1998) led me to daily self-awareness time, teaching Canadian history as beginning in Aboriginal pre-contact time, career awareness and science that originated in Native legends and stories. I concentrated on skills development and I determined to pursue quality rather than quantity while operating within the Ontario Curriculum guidelines. Eber Hampton's "twelve standards for Indian education: spirit, service, diversity, culture, tradition, respect, history, relentlessness, vitality, conflict, place and transformation" (Hampton 1995 in Battiste and Barman 1998:19-

42) were imbedded in the curriculum. As principal and full time teacher I was able to exert influence in grades Pre-K to Grade 8 during twelve years. Children were coached in the development of their spirituality through gratitude, acknowledgement of traditions that change in presentation but remain intact, balance inherent in diversity if equality is accepted, how respect is shown to all of creation, approaches to deal with racism based in knowledge of history and practice of spirituality, belief in capability and a future that may be different from their non-Native peers but not less important in the eyes of Creator and community, and what I considered most important, the development of relentlessness, place, and vitality to ensure independence.

I had modified the curriculum to be as wholistic and culturally relevant as possible within the confines of a colonized, Christian, Native community. Quantity based outcomes were changed to an emphasis on skills development. Growth in the spiritual, emotional, intellectual and physical elements of self was the expectation. At the primary level, content included pre-contact history wherein children could learn to be comfortable with their identity as a Native person and learn excellent life skills. After years of experience I learned that colonial history can only be endured after inner strength has been developed through spirituality and internalization of pride in ancestry. Canadian Native history is morose. It can only add to the intergenerational trauma of Native students who study it at whatever age (CAAS 2002:36, 43; Smith 1999:146). I discovered that anger and depression were most often the outcome of teaching such tragedy without prior preparation.

I was reminded of this at Trent University (2000-2002) where I observed young Native students overwhelmed with sadness, hurt and anger in their attempt to learn their history after fourteen years (pre-kindergarten to grade twelve) of education that denied it. Unfortunately, with no exposure to psychological understanding of trauma they are unprepared for the pain in Native Canadian history. Unless they had substantial academic and emotional support, they dropped out. "Every relationship of domination, of exploitation, of oppression, is by definition violent – in such a relationship, dominator and dominated alike are reduced to things – the former dehumanized by an excess of power, the latter by lack of it" (Friere 2000 b):10) and for those drawn to Native Studies, the violence was repeated. Despite the efforts of a Native literacy program to form a partnership to help Native Studies students cope with the emotional impact, the university failed to cooperate and efforts were abandoned.

HEALING IN RELEVANT CURRICULUM

Twenty-one years of teaching Primary Methods to Native adults during summer sessions of the Native Classroom Assistant Diploma Program (NCADP) at Nipissing University, North Bay (1984 to 2004), sustained and continues to sustain my reflections on relevant curriculum for the Native learner (Castellano et al 2000:163, 211). During those years I have spent extra hours tutoring students with literacy needs. For the last four years it has been a paid position and Nipissing University is now considering making literacy training available for all Native students attending this faculty.

NCADP students are encouraged to see each child as being a gift and having a gift and the adult's responsibility is to assist the child in finding out what that is. McCaskill in his article "Revitalization of Indian Culture: Indian Cultural Survival Schools" (Barman et al 1994: 153-179) and Monture-Angus (1995: 77-88) Mohawk Professor of Law in her chapter "Alienation and Isolation: Patterns of Colonialism in Canada's Education System" further support and explain this concept. School and individual visioning should control the opportunities provided keeping in mind those resources must be able to take the child far out in the world and the universe, especially when the communities are so isolated and technology creates such rapid growth and development. Too many Native students approach high-school education without a vision (of their gift) and in the end this affects their career choice. Many Native literacy learners arrive at programs with no vision as well. One of the reasons they express is that they have never been led to believe in their capabilities. Another is lack of confidence.

In North Bay, NCADP students are taught that there is a natural progression in learning and textbooks don't always follow it. Very few learners can cope with the rapid change of topic that textbooks and quantity based curriculum demand. During my years in education and literacy I have not found curriculum that accommodates learners who take twice as long or twice as much practice. Despite the title, Ministry of Education is not an expert in the education process. It is dominated by government and politics (Adams 1999: 40). Starting with the Common Curriculum, the ministry began subtracting basic learning processes seemingly in attempts to increase the content; a reasonable assumption when one can find 433 school year expectations for grade one; 439 for grade three; and 575 for grade eight (Ministry of Education 2001). Interestingly enough for each grade there are only an average of 65 expectations for English yet literacy levels show only a small improvement. Repetition, drill, memorization, phonetics, Uninterrupted Sustained Silent Reading, and religion were some of the tools removed. Wholistic approaches to literacy recommend putting them back. The speed, quantity and pure content that dominate education now are defeating many individuals. There is very little accommodation for learners other than those who are highly motivated, memory efficient and wealthy. Indeed, it has been my experience as an instructor in adult literacy to assist grade nine to grade twelve graduates in numeracy, reading and writing. Our discussions reveal that for many, they have been pushed out of the system in response to their impatience with a system that totally blames them for their inability to learn. Individuals who did not respond well to changes in education are the adult learners in literacy; coming to literacy because they cannot help their young children with their schoolwork and they recognize the reality of illiteracy.

In terms of methodology, NCADP students are taught three basic tenets: 1) demonstration is more effective than lecturing; teacher and child working side by side is more encouraging (Williams and Wyatt in Barman 1994: 211). 2) Native children are capable of much greater achievements if the expectations are high enough. 3) There is no such thing as a "behaviour kid" (non-compliant). There is however, a predictable negative response to ineffective teaching (Friere1985:13; Haley and Davidson 2000).

It is demonstrated to the NCADP students that Native students can learn the academic skills they need by hearing, discussing, reading, and writing about the original organization and history of their ancestors. Pride, dignity and hope are thus established. In addition, their Native students reach the understanding that they too will be leaders in their community and there are skills to be learned. Required skills have to be identified and offered. Those skills must include the pre-requisite skills and knowledge that make the transition from community to higher learning institutions achievable. In other words, survival (life) skills must be provided (Friere1985:14; Adams 1999:39). Often the NCADP students are learning the same lessons for themselves.

Each three-summer program at NCADP provides me with feedback and confirmation that holistic curriculum builds self-confidence; independence; self-esteem; and academic achievement as stated in Eber Hampton's "Redefinition of Indian Education" (in Battiste and Barman1998: 5-46). Marlene Brant Castellano Mohawk Professor Emeritus Trent University and former Co-Director of Research for the Royal Commission on Aboriginal Peoples, explains the foundation in her essay "Updating Aboriginal Traditions of Knowledge" (in Dei et al 2000: 21-34). Students return each year with stories of success after using strategies they have been taught on course: teaching responsibility as a precursor for independence; using Uninterrupted Sustained Silent Reading (USSR) not only to calm children down but to give them ample time to develop reading skills and to teach responsibility; to use maps and pictures to take the children beyond the boundaries of their community; to provide a "vision" through career awareness; self-awareness to develop pride in their ancestry; formal printing lessons and the Phonovisual Method (Phonovisual 1978) of teaching phonics to develop independence in reading and writing. During their time in North Bay, I take the opportunity to increase general literacy in social, political, spiritual and academic schemas, which affect the lives of Native people across Canada (Friere 2000 a): 47, 79). Unfortunately, when they try my methods some run into the same lateral violence I did; impacts of colonization and oppression, (Adams 1999: 52-57, Freire1985: 16, 48, Barman et al 1994: 43-62). The extent and basis of the violence executed in "broken communities where traditional virtues have eroded to the point that power and fear [drive] the community (Ross 1996:204) are narrated in class upon their return for their second year. NCADP educators are "intimidated into silence by people on the reserve who resist change" (Long and Dickason 2000: 281). Indeed, several have been removed from their school system but they persist proving once again that resiliency, vitality and relentlessness remain. I "take pride in our warriors, and our teachers are warriors for the life of our children." (Hampton in Battiste and Barman 1998:32)

POST COLONIALISM A MISLEADING NOTION THAT CREATES BARRIERS

Colonial thinking and euro-western domination of theory and policy will thwart Native capacity building (Friere1985: 17). Not only is the worldview different but institutions have been devised to protect it and educational facilities appear to be the strongest (Friere1985; Hampton "First Nations-Controlled University Education in Canada" in Castellano et al 2000:214; Battiste and Barman 1998: 208-223; Smith 1999:129). Through their dominance of research, I see knowledge creating institutions not only as the controllers of policy but also as on-going purveyors of Native stereotypes (Chrisjohn, young and Maraun 1997: 238-247, Barman et al 1987:5-6, Friere1985: 48, Miller 2004: preface). This is particularly true in literacy where policy continues to be set by academics in mainstream institutions who apparently hang onto the notion that euro-western values are the only worthy ones and who can't comprehend the Native literacy field's right to oppose an integrated version of Anglophone. Evidence can be found in damming evaluations of movements towards Native curriculum in the last twenty years. Because of the five-year comprehensive school evaluations that the Department of Indian Affairs requires for funding purposes many Native systems have returned to Non-Native staff and curriculum.

Literacy programs are shut down when research that identifies a need for wholistic training is applied. Paulo Friere explains how the wholistic literacy is counterproductive to dominance (Friere1985: 23), which helps to explain why programs get shut down when they promote critical thinking and independence.

Pre 2000, NCADP principals had full control over staffing and standards. When communities discontinued funding non-diploma programs, Nipissing University made it a diploma program taking total control of NCADP as a seemingly inevitable result. Staffing based on economics resulted in fewer Native instructors because the university didn't want to pay residence and travel costs. Prior to this, instructors were teachers, principals, and special education consultants in Native communities, keeping the content current and applicable. Now content is based on current thought in education as opposed to need: curriculum controlled by teacher bias and book theory as described in Friere's "nutritionist concept of knowledge" (Friere1987/xvi). "Eat this. It's good for you." In other words you can't know what's best. We know what's best. Our way is the right way. As I watch the flow of non-Native instructors, simplistic curriculum and stereotypical treatment of Native adult students I can only hope that my little bit of Native content creates a degree of balance. Our students are once again being treated to someone else's consciousness as if theirs was "an empty space" to be filled. (Friere 1985: 45-47)

Prior to 2000 staff recognized the diversity in student population and different Native, community contexts. Student and community needs were an integral part of programming. Post 2000, when all regulations regarding residence and standards became university driven community relevance disappeared. Instructors are now required to impress Ontario College of Teacher's evaluations for the Education Quality and Accountability Office (EQAO). More significantly, the university began to accept all graduates of NCADP into the Aboriginal Teacher Certification Program (ATCP) despite clarification by two long standing Native instructors, that those individuals, who are a step above the learners in literacy, are trained only to be the best classroom assistant possible. They are specifically supported through NCADP and most are dedicated and do excellent work under supervision. If graduation from NCADP is used as a prerequisite to ATCP, it will create another barrier to improvement in Native communities because students in NCADP will have to have a general grade twelve diploma to get in and most do not.

My thirty-four years of experience in Native Education at all levels teaches me that Native progress will always be met by a mainstream mechanism of defense (Adams 1999:147, Smith 1999: 72). The adoption of the word holistic is a form of defense. "Wholistic" has a particular meaning for Native educators and it involves community more than materialism (Hill 1999:33, Barman et al 1987:154, Castellano 2000: 8, Chrisjohn et al 1997:285, Battiste and Barman1998). Wholistic literacy involves "more than reading, numeracy and writing towards gaining access to mainstream...It is an approach to learning and languaging that begins a process of reflective and reflexive 'critical' thinking that sees problems in terms of their potential solutions". (Antone et al 2003:13) Further, the Native literacy field has recognized "a connection between Aboriginal literacy, healing community development and self-determination" for many years. (Gaikezheyongai 2000: 6) "Within the literacy field itself; 'community' suggests understanding literacy issues, and doing literacy work in the context of communities rather than as a centrally defined schooling" (Darville 1992). Government however, appears to use 'community' as a means of dispersing responsibility and costs. (Darville 1992) The adoption of holistic has made it difficult to lobby for "wholistic" Native literacy when MTCU claims they are already. Interestingly enough I can find documentation of holistic only in 1. Special Education: Planning for Independence 2. Practical Nursing Standard: Approaches to Program Design, www.edu.gov. on.ca (25 November 2004).

ILLITERACY: A LACK OF EFFECTIVE EDUCATION/SOCIALIZATION/LITERACY

My current work as an instructor in literacy confirms my reflections that the education system denies the poor, disabled, and Native populations full access to the requirements for post-secondary education. In fact, the Ontario Ministry of Education Memorandum #127 now categorically denies this same population access to an Ontario Secondary School Diploma (OSSD) because of the reading and writing (literacy) requirements. General knowledge (literacy) required to fulfill the four writing assignments in turn requires full access to Internet and/or library. Relative to rising poverty this cannot be considered universal access to education. Families living in poverty, which is most of the Native population, cannot afford computers and programming. Barriers like this deny this population the option of lifestyle improvement. Actors in this scenario are less likely to participate in social action needed for changing social policy (Friere1985, 2000 a).

In 2001, I began tutoring elementary school dropouts and grade twelve Special Education graduates through Literacy Basic Skills (LBS) level three communications, LBS level five being approximately grade eight. Two years later the emphasis has become tutoring through the General Educational Development (GED) testing program. The GED makes it possible for qualified individuals to earn a high school credential. To date, each of my clients has struggled through a system that either identified him/her with a learning disability or ignored the possibility and simply labeled the individual a "behaviour" problem (Haley and Davidson 2000: 52-56). In either of the cases, governmental attitude and lack of resources denies effective access to full education.

Ineffective education is the norm in Native communities; a result of generations of rejection of Native worldview and history and government control (Grant 1996: 88, 89,103). Native literacy now suffers the same fate even as it attempts to support individuals who failed as a result of lack of resources.

I bring all of this learning to my work as a literacy worker as I continue my constant involvement in the Native community. It is the combination of all of these experiences that provides me with a unique lens through which to analyze literacy and theorize a definition for Native literacy. I reiterate Michael Hart's statement, "These experiences have shaped me. I have come to certain beliefs very strongly" (Hart 2002:19). It is through the use of my personal experience, reflective teaching and strategy building, that I bring forward my definition of Native literacy.

NATIVE LITERACY REVOLUTIONIZED

The misfit between Native literacy and the people it serves is a continuation of past and present educational practices in the Native community (Barman et al1994:167, Ponting1986: 260-281, Friere 1985: 8). In as much as Native communities share a similar history, diverse needs and cultural expression in the six hundred- thirty-three Native communities across Canada, dictate that each community create their own materials (Barman et al 1994:155, Friere 1985:12). Manifest destiny and white privilege still describe the dominance of one worldview and must be acknowledged and confronted not only by the Aboriginal community/literacy but also by policy makers (Shore 2003:19-25, Kendall 2001:1-10). Policy and procedure, outcomes and standards in literacy continue to be prescribed by euro-western world-view through the Ministry of Training, Colleges and Universities (MTCU) and Anglophone literacy stream through the Ontario Literacy Coalition (OLC).

The Ontario Native Literacy Coalition and the twenty-six programs it represents accept as their mission, the empowerment of the people. In general, "to empower means to enhance our ability to control our own lives, or to develop a sense of collective influence over the social conditions of one's life. At the individual level this can mean drawing on inner strength to take control of a situation and assert one-self. Interpersonally it can mean sharing resources for mutual benefit or working together co-operatively". (Ristock and Pennell 1996:1, 2) In actuality, Native literacy cannot empower people through a system that begins at employment rather than self-development (Folinsbee 2000: 19-25, Friere 1985:10). It must change to address all four elements of self in order to empower. As Native literacy currently exists, it is simply a continuation of assimilation tactics that have long since been proven wrong and damaging to the Native population (Miller 2004:271, Kuhn & Sweetman, Chrisjohn et al 1997:272-273, Boldt 1993:61).

The literature on Residential schools, Native Education, Native History and Native Literacy describe Native wholistic literacy training as development in four areas: spiritual (identity, self-concept, self-worth, and self-esteem); emotional (acknowledgement of history and cultural differences); physical (acknowledgement of history, environment, health and nutrition); intellectual (literature, history, current social schemas, and academics). These are stated needs of Aboriginal people (Barman et al 1994: 157,168). All of the literature points to a relationship between history, needs and solutions (Barman et al 1994: 213, Adams 1999:139); all related to Canadian Native history in terms of the attempt at genocide through the Canadian Indian residential school era (Friere1985: 48, Crosson-Tower 1999: 95, 105, CRRF 2000: 36).

Native individuals must have the opportunity to know their pre-contact history. They too are victims of stereotyping and misrepresentation of Native culture and worldview and their healing lies not just in acknowledging it but in programs that compensate for the deprivation caused by it (Barman et al 1994:155, Adams 1999: 42, Kirkness and Bowman 1992: 103). Native literacy learners have more than employability concerns to overcome. Their needs are deeper, long-standing and foundational to their ability to learn. Needs for identity, belongingness, and confidence carried forward into adult life must be met in order to improve post-secondary achievement for Native students and to provide motivation to further education for literacy learners (Middleton-Moz 1989). There are essential needs that need to be addressed to free the Native learner to learn (Hill 1995:53, Cockell and Penny 2001:39-40). These needs are long-standing, intergenerational and identified in research yet unknown or unavailable to Native literacy workers.

FOUR ORIGINS OF NEEDS

1. Intergenerational trauma, the impact of residential schools is a truth (Barman, Hebert, McCaskill 1999, Chrisjohn et al 1997, Milloy 1999, Grant 1996: 223, Boldt 1994: 61, Miller 2004: 271, Crosson-Tower 1999: 364, Knockwood 1994:156). Logically, the impacts of that trauma must be addressed in literacy programs as it

is not addressed in formal education systems (Horsman 1999:169-214). Native students continue to leave formal education prior to completion. Despite years of statistics that have identified the issue there has been no substantial improvement. The RCAP Report, Literature in Native Education and literature by Native authors identify causes: denial of basic human needs of identity, self-concept, self-worth and self-esteem in the system; policy that prevents social action (Barman et al 1994: 64, 213-223, Chrisjohn et al 1997: 252, Adams 1999: 55, 81, 145). Oppression and colonization and the effect they have had on Native identity must be addressed (Adams 1999: 86,149). Identity depends on knowing where you come from, knowing where you are and where you are going (Middleton-Moz 1989: 23, Haig-Brown 1998: 279-282, Barman et al 1994:39, 40). Native literacy cannot cooperate in denying Native history and worldview, not when it is identified as part of empowerment of Native people (Adams 1999:147).

Acknowledging the trauma is step one (Middleton-Moz 1989:1-18, Chrisjohn et al 1997:110). Do we require Native psychiatrists/psychologists to begin the process? Yes we need trained individuals but certification has endorsed another barrier, a disbelief in our own power (Chrisjohn et al 1997:295, Monture-Angus 1995:77). For as long as Native people adopt that disbelief, healing in the communities will continue to be stifled. As Monture -Angus states, "If you do not have that little piece of paper that signifies the end of your education it does not mean you know nothing. Education is also about understanding our real life experiences in both our hearts and minds" (Monture-Angus 1995:83)

Native individuals are entitled to know that their behaviour, attitudes and values are a result of abusive conditioning through the education system past and present (Chrisjohn et al 1997: 257, Newman 1994:137-144). Freedom to understand that it is not an innate lack of capability that prevents the Native population from higher education and achievement is empowering. Understanding the inter-generational, psychological impact of residential school trauma validates feelings of lack of control and hopelessness both of which are responses to oppression (Crosson-Tower 1999: 95,105,364,

Middleton-Moz 1989: 149). It re-presents a vision of hope (Barman et al 1994: 158, Crosson-Tower 1999: 398-411). This is what Native Literacy can begin to provide, to effect social change for the Native community.

Sharing in education and literacy allowed me to witness the individual empowerment in knowing that the problem is a society that refuses to acknowledge the potential of a population it has been conditioned to believe is "lazy, irresponsible, and simple"(Barman et al 1994:157, 1999:119, Boldt 1994:15-19, Adams 1999: 23). Knowing this helps the learner buy into literacy training but there are so many issues besides curriculum and policy that progress is painfully slow. Change to the status quo is not going to happen through the schools nor will it happen with the current definition of Native literacy. But it could happen for future generations if Native literacy gains the freedom to adopt its own definition under current funding.

2. The Indian Act and treaties, physically, socially, politically and intellectually isolate Native communities. Canadian society remains a functionally foreign land to many Native people. The Indian Act now allows residents to leave their reserves and access Canadian society but inadequate funding often contributes to community education systems that do not overcome barriers to successful transition (Barman et al 1994:159, Friere1985: 49, Chrisjohn et al 1997:272). For example: I was contracted to do a Dokis First Nation Curriculum Review in 2004. I saw the Department of Indian Affairs requirement of "minimal" evidence of provincial curriculum as a continuing policy of substandard education for Native people. When all Native students have to leave the home community either for secondary or post-secondary education it is essential that they own an efficient level of education. Culture and role shock are enough to deal with without academic issues (Barman et al 1994: 44, Deloria Jr. 1997: 7).

Native communities gained "Local Control of Education" (Chrisjohn et al 1997: 268-272) but not the funding, resulting in continued lack of quality resources (Barman et al 1994: 37-40, 48, 68-73). Insufficient funding denies the communities relevant programming and the fallout appears in Native literacy programs where the same issues appear. Aboriginal individuals across the country - 68.5% (RCAP1996, VOL.3: 445) – have been caught up in the need for a grade twelve diploma for employment. Provided they can overcome the same personal, situational and institutional barriers they confronted when attending high school they can achieve a grade twelve equivalency through the **G**eneral **E**ducation **D**evelopment Testing (GED) Program. Issues such as: poverty, isolation, lack of information, undiagnosed disabilities, low self-esteem, family attitudes and priorities still have to be addressed. Institutional barriers such as: admission criteria, lack of vocational counseling, absence of bicultural staff, lack of cross-cultural sensitivity, general discrimination and racism, and a tendency of educational programs to not take culture into account still remain (Hill 1995:53).

3. Language barriers unrecognized, deny effective communication (Castellano, Davis, Lahache 2000:19, 23, Hampton in Battiste 1999:4, Kuhn and Sweetman (2002: 21, 25, Ross 1996:101-130, Spielman1998: 233-239, Friere 2000: 21) in most arenas that involve mainstream and Native participants. During discussions with MTCU officials and consultants, Native literacy practitioners, elders and social workers it is clear that at any given time there are several levels of miscommunication happening. For example, the difference between "evaluation and inspection" (Friere 1985: 23) has just been observed in the Native literacy field. Practitioners were expecting ideas and support during annual evaluation visits while MTCU consultants were merely "policing' or making inspections. Over the two years I have been on the Ontario Native Literacy Coalition (ONLC) board, the coalition has been actively advocating for cultural sensitivity training for the MTCU consultants. Practitioners began voicing concerns to ONLC in 2004 to the effect that they were feeling intimidated, like the "police" had arrived in their program (Oct.2004 AGM Report). There is no recognition on the part of MTCU, of the reality that Native literacy practitioners must function in: some programs are urban stand-a-lone making them completely independent while the majority of the programs are under the authority of a friendship center executive director or a

band administrator representing Chief and Council. This translates into lack of timely communication, planning, focus and finances. The rigidity of timelines and guidelines create an issue of rapid staff turnover, which make the situation even worse. Monitoring visits to enforce the guidelines and that can lead to closure of a program often subject even the stand-a-lone practitioner to severe stress. Aboriginal community based programs have two bosses – local friendship centre Executive Director or chief and council, then MTCU and Ministry officials who refuse to acknowledge this fact in their visits. At a meeting I attended with MTCU in Toronto, the executive officers joked about what Dan Kay, the supervisor of consultants would do if ever he found out that a consultant assisted a practitioner in his/her administration. Many of the Native literacy practitioners are new every year. There appears to be no support for them. Research and requests for a field support worker who can provide ideas and support for the programs is repeatedly denied despite research that proves a need (Antone et al 2003, Logan-Elliott and McClain 2003).

Understanding of English varies by location and the understood schemas of the individual. At any one time several definitions of the words "healing", "support", or "traditional" can be operating amongst Native individuals in one room. I see this as another of the impacts of history in the Native community. It appears that more than language has been lost in the translation from Native languages to English. The environment of the change altered meanings creating misunderstandings even amongst Native communities (Spielmann 1998, Ross 1996, Maracle 1996: 39). In fact, Native literacy is the fourth Native organization I have noted this in. I have brought it to the attention of staff at NCADP, Niijkiwendidaa Anishnaabe-Kwewag Services Circle, Ontario Native Literacy Coalition and the Anishnawbe Health Toronto: Homeless Unit. Vocabulary such as healing path or journey, counseling, manager, training, staff development, cultural sensitivity can have different meanings for different Aboriginal individuals without the input of non-Aboriginal consultants, instructors, managers and executive directors. Stereotypes of Aboriginal learners and clients have a significant effect on language and policy used in organizations. While different levels of education create one level of mis-communication that tends to alienate Aboriginal people from each other, at another level different communities have not only different meanings for words but they also have differing rules of discourse. One repercussion of this often unrecognized barrier is a very literal, "in-the-box", and interpretation of the English language thwarting cooperative action to change the status quo. An example would be a strategic planning session I attended during which heated discussions began to happen because of a discrepancy of understanding between the executive director and staff over the concept of "open communication". The executive director had healing circles (counseling) in mind while staff had interpersonal airing of problems and differences. In the end it became necessary to explain that the organization cannot or should not be counseling its own employees.

Additionally, MTCU officials use only vocabulary that appears in policy and documents; an underlying strategy of oppression (Chrisjohn et al 1997:303, Freire 1985:8-9, 23). As President of the ONLC board, I observed that when the discrepancy in understanding is raised, MTCU officials don't comprehend the significance. Neither they nor most Native practitioners recognize that non-compliance issues in their evaluations may simply be the result of differing translations. My conclusion is again: a solution to the ongoing oppression through the use of language will have to be explored by the Native literacy field (Friere 1985: 8, 17, 39, 51).

In the eighties, speech and language testing at Cape Croker labeled almost 95% of the kindergarten, language delayed. At the time it was noted that the test itself was not relevant to the Native population (Castellano et al 2000:161). While that was true, it begs the question, should the test be revised or should vocabulary and language be built to reach the level of the dominant society? My experience and the history of Native education suggest that the requisite communications skills (literacy) must be a large part of the education process. I agree that "despite all of our differences [the] education system [is] a site for future change" (Monture-Angus

1995: 69). Under the new definition, Native literacy could not only assist but also be an advocate in this huge endeavor.

4. Euro-western paradigms skew concepts and attitudes towards a capitalist society rather than individual self-development (Friere 1985:26, 31, Chrisjohn et al 1997: 5, 90). Currently enforced standards and outcomes of minimum pay employment create continual opposition in the Native literacy field. Because of the "white privilege" influence literacy materials require modification. The dedicated people in Native literacy are not trained teachers, yet adapting, modifying, and accommodating are formal education concepts that they are required to practice. In fact, when I studied the learning outcomes matrix for the sake of the learner assessments, as an elementary school teacher I recognized that it is taken directly from school curriculum documents. Practitioners may not understand the terminology much less have the time, space, or funds to efficiently perform these activities. Additionally, curriculum documents are guided by colonial attitudes that fail to acknowledge and allow a worldview that embraces wholistic training. Collective, survival-based skills founded in spirituality are ignored despite ample needs studies (Barman et al 1994:162). There can be no doubt that "silencing" continues. An espoused definition of wholistic Native literacy will empower Native learners to speak out and "there is an important connection between overcoming silencing and ending collective exclusion. It is much easier to exclude a silent so-called minority, than a vocal one." (Monture-Angus 1995: 29)

CONTENT: THE COMPELLING TOOL

In 2004, few, including Native Peoples, can fully understand the concept of holistic, Native socialization. The term holistic, now adopted by many confounds the Aboriginal concept of wholistic. Easy to do, considering Canada's early acts of genocide towards Aboriginal people (Milloy 1999, Chrisjohn et al 1997: 256-258) and indeed this author sees the adoption of the term in the last ten years as part of the disruption of Aboriginal resurgence (Friere 2000 a):11, Chrisjohn et al 1997:66).

Pre-contact, Native life-training began at birth and ended at death indicating that they already incorporated life-long learning, one of the objectives of an MTCU funded LBS program. Training was wholistic; the outcome was collective. Individuals were assisted in developing individual strength for the power and survival of the community. Training included: spiritual guidance; academic guidance; health and physical development; social/emotional development. No component of life was ignored. The individual simultaneously grew to be strong, confident and independent yet dependent on the interconnectedness of all parts of the earth. The stories and teachings through which this was accomplished are at the same time beautiful, soothing and informative. Lessons were shared and education was both a family and community affair (Barman et al 1994: 3, 1999: 26).

This information is still unavailable to most Native individuals in their own community. My theory is that historical content can be used to tutor in communications and self-direction/self-management in literacy program. Reading, writing and discussion of this content can accomplish not just LBS outcomes but outcomes that address known needs in the Aboriginal community (Literacy Alberta 2004, Canadian Council on Social Development 1988: 59-75). Furthermore, literature written by Native authors and research by ethical Native and non-Native researchers must be the source. The inclusion of this material will accomplish more than one thing. Respect, understanding and several communications skills can be addressed while acknowledgement and healing of old hurts will provide motivation to reach higher both in academics and lifestyle. This of course must steer the next era in Native literacy project proposals; creation of relevant learning materials; freedom to provide Native wholistic literacy programming and employment of field support for the twenty-six isolated Native literacy programs.

CONCLUSION

Native literacy programs exist to assist those who have not reached their potential. Native literacy programs mandated to provide basic literacy skills, must address Native specific needs. Current rhetoric about self-direction, self-motivation and essential skills, appears to create a venue through which to address the identified spiritual, emotional intellectual and physical needs of the Native individual. Native literacy defined as a continuum of relevant guidance that sets in motion the healing of the psychological impact of Native history and provides individual and community access to skills development that increases self-determination, will meet these needs (Boldt 1993: xvi)

CHAPTER 5
SUMMARY AND CONCLUSIONS

SUMMARY

To combat a common misunderstanding created by the title Native literacy, it was necessary to analyze two fields of literacy - Ontario literacy and Native literacy in Ontario and their relationship. Chapter three clarified that Native literacy is only a title and does not embrace Native learning style, worldview or community reality. Chapter four's concentration on Aboriginal worldview presented compelling grounds to construct a specific definition for Native literacy. Policies that are created on the basis of urban Anglophone statistics cannot address the needs of Aboriginal individuals who do not have access to the same services as learners in urban centers. Further, clarity of the true direction of Native literacy is essential if Native literacy is to access sufficient support and funding to carry out its responsibility to Aboriginal learners and communities. The Ministry of Training, Colleges and Universities demands outcomes in response to government driven policy. Minimum basic funding that is administrated makes those policies appear trivial in that it creates situations of insufficient manpower, supplies, equipment and time. Sufficient funding is required to allow Native literacy to fully meet the unique needs of the Aboriginal community that will in turn create social justice for the Aboriginal population but the immediate issue is the right and freedom to observe wholistic Native literacy.

As pointed out in chapter two, literacy cannot claim a precise definition. However, the general population accepts literacy as simply learning to read and write while the Ministry of Training, Colleges and Universities (MTCU) defines it as reading, writing and numeracy. In recent years, the definition has unofficially changed again to mean reading, writing and numeracy for employment. The disconnection between literacy and basic skills and employability has created dissatisfaction and stress in the literacy field in response to the oppression of learners. Learners endure complete control of their lives at the hands of government services whose only goal is to get them off welfare and into low paying jobs in complete disregard for individuality and family. Individuals are expected to work or job search and attend literacy despite the fact that they have young families and no money for child care or transportation and often it is a case of a one-parent family. Government's one-sided economic goals appear to deny poverty and its pervasive effects on lives.

Chapter two also discussed the high practitioner turnover rate a repercussion of a single-minded focus on employment and accountability. Input of front line workers (practitioners) has little or no impact on policy. As one practitioner pointed out, policy is made and then practitioners get a few weeks to comment.

In chapter three, Native literacy was clarified as a division of Ontario literacy with no allowance for differentiation from the mainstream. Despite research, documents, articles and books that expose the intergenerational damage of history and residential schools - the foundation of need in Aboriginal communities - Native literacy struggles with the same issues as the Francophone, Anglophone and Deaf streams in terms of guidelines, outcomes and funding. Francophone, Anglophone and Deaf streams however do not have the intergenerational damage to overcome. Workforce literacy is now expected to be the main thrust of literacy in Aboriginal communities as it across Ontario.

However, research cited in chapter four identified the absence of employment opportunities that the majority of Aboriginal communities endure. Stats Canada and Aboriginal surveys expose a huge unemployed population on reserve a large proportion of which includes individuals with insufficient or incomplete education. This study proposes that Native literacy efforts to alleviate insufficient general knowledge and skills at two transition points – high-school and postsecondary – would assist Aboriginal individuals to successfully integrate into the mainstream via more appropriate education opportunities - opportunities that would later end in employment.

Chapter four presented an argument for a different definition of Native literacy, one that is more effective in the Aboriginal community. Wholistic Native literacy is presented as a response to the need for healing - not only history - but the continuing, alienating, formal education of Aboriginal children and youth. Alienation in the form of Aboriginal youth's ignorance of identity influences and sufficient skills that accompany them when they leave the security of their reserve to be fully integrated with mainstream attitude, racism, and worldview of materialism and success based on hierarchy. An explanation of how education has separated 'what we study from how we live' can be found on page seventy-two in Diane Hill's thesis, *Holistic learning: A Model of Education Based on Aboriginal Cultural Philosophy*. In the case of Aboriginal individuals, we have spent more than 500 years learning how other people live, how they achieve success and how they become dominant. What we learn rarely applies to us and will continue to defeat us if Indian Affairs policies continue to be imposed on us – policies that over a period of time have become the origin of systemic (latent) racism and outright prejudice. The resultant adoption of white privilege maintains the oppression.

The arrival of western, European worldview had a profound influence on the original inhabitants of the Americas; the North American Aboriginal nations. Over a period of four centuries the strength of a patriarchal, hierarchal culture overpowered Aboriginal worldview. However, Aboriginal worldview has adapted and survived despite legislation, laws, forced relocation, and attempted cultural genocide but this knowledge and validation is not readily available to most communities much less individuals.

Further, within the last ten to fifteen years the profoundly negative influence of colonialism and oppression has been recorded by Aboriginal people within academic, historical, sociological, philosophical, medical and literary ranks. Yet, policy specifically for Aboriginal peoples to free themselves and move forward is denied. A review of literature uncovers a persistent, resilient Aboriginal philosophy of socialization that endures within every nation despite the British North American Act, The Indian Act, the Department of Indian Affairs, and Federal and Provincial governments and Ministries. The needs studies are complete, the curriculum is apparent – all that is needed now is the funding to put curriculum into print and policy that allows putting it into action.

Conclusions

In Ontario literacy – Anglophone, Francophone, DEAF and Native literacy - practitioners who work face to face with the recipients of literacy training advocate for more life-skills and less employment readiness in literacy guidelines. Additionally, literacy needs must be seen as equally important as formal education and garner better support from all other services available to Ontario residents. "Literacy policies need to be embedded in all social, economic and cultural policies. Policies affecting employment and skills training, healthcare, childcare, law, and taxation as well as those affecting education have an impact on literacy. Literacy in the knowledge age has many dimensions, encompassing much more than the ability to read and write" (CAE 2003). The Ministry of Training, Colleges and Universities (MTCU) and the National Literacy Secretariat (NLS) appear to be operating outside of this education and life-skills understanding of literacy. The employability focus taken by the MTCU abandons the necessary foundation to learning that is needed for those learners whom Judith Coleman speaks of in her 2003 paper *Education in Ontario: Education Resources and the Mental Health of Children and Youth*. Coleman advocates for special needs learners in the formal education system of whom "50% had behavioural problems among their exceptionalities" (Coulman 2003: 9). These same learners appear in the possible 30% of learners in literacy, who have learning disabilities (OLC 2001). My experience is that many children labeled behavioural are individuals who have learned very early that they cannot function without support and they aren't going to get it. In light of the 30% of literacy learners having learning disabilities the degree of funding on Workforce literacy appears to be misplaced. It would be better spent on providing sufficient funding for resources in literacy so that adult learners forced into literacy through the Ontario Works/Welfare Assistance Program do not meet with a repeat of their childhood experience in school. Furthermore, literacy workers can be seen to have a responsibility similar to special education resource teachers and counselors with little or no training in either of these fields.

Native education, "Indian control of Indian education" has existed since 1972, Native literacy since 1988. So, why is there still only a 4% post-secondary completion rate amongst Aboriginal people? Why does the 88% unemployment rate in Aboriginal society fail to change? Not only has the real source of the problem - intergenerational impact of cultural genocide – not been exposed but the solution has once again been researched, organized and mandated by an "outside" influence (Smith 1999: 7, 20) in the form of the Ministry of Training, Colleges and Universities (MTCU), the National Literacy Secretariat (NLS) and the Ontario Literacy Coalition (OLC).

My experience as a board member and president of the Ontario Native Literacy Coalition (ONLC) and this research have clarified the insidious and pervasive control over literacy practice and expected outcomes exercised by government. ONLC unwittingly as it may be is part of that control. Research paradigms guided by MTCU, NLS and OLC cannot meet the needs of Aboriginal people and have put the control outside of this population. One example of the effect of this control is to be found in Ken Hill's (2001) statement.

> "If cultural knowledge and skills are to become the end (outcome) and the content is to serve as the means to that end then the content itself should be organized around processes for acquiring cultural knowledge and skills. In a culture-based curriculum therefore, cultural elements should be reflected in the content so that what is taught is consistent with the goal toward which the teaching is directed. One way by which this may be accomplished is to replace the traditional list of academic subjects with a list

of appropriate general cultural learning areas and devise an educational system aimed at developing an understanding of these cultural learning areas." (Hill 2001: 31)

Ken Hill's statement describes an education system more than Native literacy, which was the purpose of the project financed by ONLC. Furthermore, it appears to incorporate the "baffle gab" of research. Clear language - language within which literacy practitioners and the people they work with operate - is not the norm for research reports. Research with its own language, a scientific language of methodology, variables, thesis, ethics and results, can sometimes appear like a curtain to hide behind when the real research appears incomplete or disconnected from the purpose. Experience with research in Native literacy has prompted the Ontario Native Literacy Coalition to shy away from further projects requiring research. Added to the negative history of research in Aboriginal communities in times past, research that uses language for the more highly educated is ineffectual. Research that uses highly technical and/or research lingo can not serve any real purpose for the Aboriginal community if the community has to depend on non-Aboriginal "consultants" to interpret it.

Further, I maintain that Ken Hill's statement for change is what holds Native literacy development at a standstill in terms of purpose and growth for two reasons. First, after generations of oppression most Aboriginal individuals (communities) are not receptive to full scale changes to systems. Culture and traditions are concepts historically punishable by government and church and continue not to be trusted (Aboriginal Healing and Wellness Strategy 2000: 75). "Dime novels and movies have defined Native Americans as "discovered by Columbus", "lurking in the wilderness", attacking wagon trains", "scalping pioneers", "savages who hindered progress", "nomadic, warlike primitive and simple" (Bataille 2001:5). Is it any wonder that Aboriginal communities would as soon ignore this history? Second, what is meant by cultural knowledge and skills? Is the curriculum that is required to operate in Canadian society included? There needed to be a much deeper explanation of how the curriculum could meet the needs of both Aboriginal communities and MTCU. The fact that ONLC published this document detracted from their aura of support even in the eyes of the Native literacy practitioners.

In her article *Sunrise: Activism and Self-determination in First Nations Education* (1972- 1998), Sharilyn Calliou refers to Marie Battiste who wrote in her chapters in *Indian Education in Canada* (Barman et al 1986, 1987) how using print literature as a "measure of literacy for peoples who have not had access to print materials" (Hylton 1999) is inappropriate. Calliou and Battiste effectively clarify this reason that MTCU is suspect in maintaining the status quo in Aboriginal communities. "The stereotype of Indians as 'illiterate savages' came about because Indians were print deprived" (Battiste 1987). Aboriginal people read – the same stereotypical text as everyone else. The fact that literacy policy doesn't fund the purchase of books or the development of materials ensures that the Aboriginal community will remain "illiterate" but only in terms of continuing to live mainstream's definition of Aboriginal people. It would be better to see Native literacy as "planting the seed" of renewal and change. Further, the literacy needs in the Aboriginal community are different. Reading and writing may not be the issue. What is often the issue is the lack of general knowledge about the world outside of the isolation of a minority, which has also been physically, economically and socially isolated from mainstream.

Literacy is part of the healing process needed to combat the intergenerational damage of history and residential schools. (Antone et al 2003, Aboriginal Healing and Wellness 2000:50-51) Aboriginal individuals have a need to understand the conditioning that has been imposed on them before they can remove the layers of oppression and allow their true spirits and identity to improve the third world conditions thy endure in their communities. Even though Rupert Ross (1996), Assistant crown Attorney for the district of Kenora, was speaking of a justice system his description of people receiving salaries; child-welfare workers, NADAP (Native Alcohol and Drug Addiction Program) workers, community health representatives, mental health workers band family service workers, nurses and teachers as players already in place for healing (Ross 1996: 221) supports my argument that Native literacy must assert its place in that journey. The wholistic meaning of Native literacy needs to be enforced. Then Native literacy can be held responsible for providing healing, wholistic literacy. The human resources are in place. The vision is not. The entire Aboriginal community needs to take responsibility for providing the resources.

Howard Adams provides further clarity about the healing journey in his statement that Aboriginal literature must reveal colonization, oppression, racism, and classism (Adams 1999:110). Native literacy can be part of that process by introducing and adapting works of Native authors to the needs of the Native literacy learner. Native literacy can be part of the team that opens doors to Native literature, original Aboriginal teachings and renewed respect, acceptance and dependence on Elders. In other words, Native literacy can be the catalyst for "giving people the teaching they need to live good lives not just escape [and return to] painful ones" (Ross 1996: 228).

As Janice Acoose endorses Emma LaRocque's statement, I too, "dream for liberation in our land…I dream for our people to stop dying, to stop feeling so alienated and so marginalized. I dream for our collective and individual well-being." (Acoose 1995:19)

The dream lies in literacy. Literacy can provide the awareness and transition to different schema including: 1. Employment –organizational psychology, protocol, responsibility, labour laws, deductions, essential skills, career opportunities, opportunity for advancement, education level required, training opportunities; 2. Post-secondary education – courses offered, level of support, five year planning, research/library skills, essay writing skills, critical reading, personal and academic support, advocacy, policy and procedure in education; and 3. Adulthood – planning, rent, insurance, savings, living expenses, parental responsibilities, owning a house/car/ property, budgeting, rights and responsibilities, compatibility, respect and honour, as well as communications.

Literacy can provide knowledge of other schema that heavily influence an individual's life; government, Indian Affairs, Indian Act, human rights, Aboriginal world view, history.

The wholistic Native literacy model described would provide opportunities for learners to; build confidence in their roles as models for their children; create relevant, culture based materials for the children of the community during the process of literacy learners speaking, reading, and writing; build their numeracy skills during the shared search to secure funds for sustaining the model; build their skills in technology while researching and publishing the cultural materials.

In effect, Native literacy would be wholistic. The Native literacy program would provide workshops to address the essential socio-economic skills needed for new high-school students and those individuals considering university and college. The employment process could be addressed in literacy while the community economic development program concentrates on accessing development dollars as opposed to training.

Employment schema, opportunities and requisite training could be researched and presented by the literacy program. For those individuals who continue to be alienated by a structured formal school setting literacy would support them through the education process to acquire the skills to achieve a GED thus effectively relieving some of the pressures of the regular school system. In other words we would be practicing prevention rather than intervention - a wholistic Native concept. The next era in Aboriginal history could move closer towards original worldview and renewed community strength through the redefinition of "Native" literacy.

Although Aboriginal peoples have not had the "enjoyment of freedom and resources" they have not sacrificed their "underlying diversity in the process." (Barsh 1994:37) Further, to their tribute, Aboriginal people have maintained the one resource that cannot be expropriated – their understanding of wholistic and all that it offers. All that is needed is the freedom to practice it in literacy.

Government policy continues to create a society that not only caters to the more fortunate but creates barriers for the less fortunate

(Hargrave 2004). Not only do practitioners struggle with helping and advocating for learners: who lose their support; are affected by classism when they do reach the point of applying to college; who suffer through the ignorance of employment agencies regarding distance, equipment and clothing needs for employment when they achieve a GED; who have internalized a mind set that doesn't allow them to say no to anything from Ontario Works; and who meet with resistance to go on to further education rather than a low paying job; but the practitioners have to side-step the Ministry of Training Colleges and Universities which strictly enforces a policy that states that advocacy is not an accepted activity of literacy. Another example of how mainstream (Anglophone) society controls can be found in the millions of dollars spent on *Train Ontario* and workforce workplace literacy resources which served to ignore and bury the real issue of insufficient human resources, equipment and materials that Native literacy workers and ONLC have documented.

"A wholistic process cannot be explained by shattering it into its component parts and adding local explanations to the segments" (Battiste and Henderson 2000:77). It would be difficult to write about a wholistic literacy process that doesn't automatically include past, present, future, and spirituality. Social, political, spiritual, academic and historical awareness must be part of the adult literacy model simply because it cannot happen for the children during the early years of literacy development. For, as long as Aboriginal children continue to, "march out from the schools...effectively re-socialized, and imbued with the values of European culture" (Hill 1999:5) there will be high unemployment and a need for wholistic Native adult literacy. With their identity: body-awareness, self-concept, self-esteem, and self-determination, deadened by a system that continues to quash their essence, Aboriginal individuals will continue to live their current quality of life. As Diane Hill states "oppressive forces external to Aboriginal communities are no longer needed to convince people that their original way of life is inappropriate. Now, individual family belief systems work to oppress other family belief systems found within the communities. Aboriginal people now oppress and oppose one another." (Hill 1999:7)

In *Protecting Indigenous Knowledge and Heritage* Battiste and Henderson propose that we envision the impossible and translate it into text." (Battiste and Henderson 2000:3). This study is written for those in Native literacy who struggle to understand why Native literacy must follow the same policy as the Anglophone and why it is so difficult to change that. It has been written to inform the Aboriginal community that changes in Native literacy needs the support of the communities; local, provincial and national Aboriginal organizations; and the Canadian public for current literacy policy affects all. If the practitioners who cannot understand research lingo cannot read or access it I have not met my personal vision of sharing what I know with my community.

This study has not only provided me with a place to express understandings based on experience, but it has also confirmed my understanding that independence of thought and action for the majority of the Aboriginal population is almost impossible in light of the concerted effort to continue the path of cultural genocide on the part of government through its ministries.

There is a vast difference between "holistic" as used by mainstream and "wholistic" as known by Aboriginal worldview. Holistic according to mainstream understanding continues to deny the spiritual and community aspect of life. Wholistic according to Aboriginal worldview understands that spirit strengthened in identity is the axis of development. Left to practice its own definition and understanding of wholistic literacy, Native literacy would make significant changes in levels of postsecondary education and employment. Wholistic Native literacy can provide an understanding of the conditioning of history thus freeing the individual from the self-fulfilling prophecy of inferiority. While it presents the long denied spiritual and community values in original Aboriginal worldview, wholistic Native literacy would quicken needed growth in Aboriginal society. Aboriginal worldview historically embraced the life-long learner concept that adult education embraces. Aboriginal worldview has always embraced individual and community responsibility to maintain community denying current individualism and politics. Additionally, Aboriginal worldview has historically embraced the interconnectedness of peoples, environment and philosophy. Therefore, when the right to heal is returned through Aboriginal definition of wholistic literacy, and Aboriginal society returns to health, mainstream too will heal and move forward.

REFERENCES

ABC Canada Literacy Foundation. *Literacy Facts: Adult Literacy in Canada*, <http://www.abc-canada.org/literacy_facts/ > (20 August 2002).

Aboriginal Canada Portal. (2003). Report on aboriginal Community Connectivity Infrastructure, <http://www.aboriginalcanada.gc.ca/acp/site.nsf/en/ao28084.html(23 February 2005)

Aboriginal Healing and Wellness Strategy. (2000). *Longitudinal Study Phase 1*. University of Toronto: Centre for Applied Social Research: Faculty of Social Work.

Acoose, J. (1995). *Iskwewak: Neither Indian Princesses Nor Easy Squaws*. Toronto: Women's Press

Adams, H. (1999). *Tortured People: the Politics of Colonization*. Penticton: Theytus Books Ltd.

Alfred, Taiaiake. 1999. *Peace Power Righteousness: an Indigenous Manifesto*. Don Mills: Oxford University Press

Anderson, D. (2003). *Business Plan National Indigenous Literacy Association*, <http://www.nald.ca/fulltext/business/13.htm> (14 August 2003).

Antone, E., Gamlin, P., Provost Turchetti, P. (2003). *Final Report Literacy and Learning: Acknowledging Aboriginal Holistic Approaches to Learning in Relation to "Best Practices" Literacy Programs*. University of Toronto: Ontario Institute for Studies in Education, <http://www.nald.ca/fulltext/aboriglt/finlrprt/cover.htm> (12 February 2005).

Antone, R., Miller, D. and Myers, B. (1986). *The Power within People*. Deseronto: Peace Tree Technologies

Archibald, J. (1998). "Locally Developed Native Studies Curriculum: an Historical and Philosophical Rationale" in Battiste and Barman *First Nations Education in Canada: The Circle Unfolds*. Vancouver: UBC Press.

Ashley D. and Orenstein D.M. (1990). *Sociological Theory: Classical Statements*. 2nd ed. Boston: Allyn and Bacon

Assembly of First Nations: Report. (1994). *Breaking the Chains: First Nation Literacy and Self Determination*. Ottawa: Assembly of First Nations.

Assembly of First Nations. (1988). *Tradition and Education: Towards a Vision of our Future*. Ottawa: National Indian Brotherhood Assembly of First Nations.

Armstrong, J. (1993). ed. *Looking at the Words of Our People: First Nations Analysis of Literature*. Penticton: Theytus Books Ltd.

Arvay, M. (1998). "Struggling with Re-presentation, Voice and Self in Narrative Research" *Connections' 98*, eds. Anderson J. and Miller C. B.C: University of Victoria (1998), <http://www.educ.uvic.ca/connections/Conn98/arvay.html>
(16 October 2004).

Barman, J., Hebert Y. and McCaskill D. (1999). eds. *Indian Education in Canada Volume 1: The Legacy*. Vancouver: UBC Press.

Barman, J., Hebert Y. and McCaskill D. (1994). eds. *Indian Education in Canada Volume 2: The challenge*. Vancouver: UBC Press.

Barsh, R.L. (1994). "Canada's Aboriginal People: Social Integration or Disintegration?" *Canadian Journal of Native Studies* 14 no.1.

Bataille, G. M. (2001). ed. *Native American Representations: First Encounters, Distorted Images, and Literary Appropriations.* Lincoln: University of Nebraska Press.

Battiste, M. (1987). "Micmac Literacy and Cognitive Assimilation" in *Indian Education in Canada Volume 1: The legacy* (1987).

Battiste, M. and Barman J. (1998). eds. *First Nations Education in Canada: the Circle Unfolds.* Vancouver: UBC Press.

Battiste, M. and Youngblood Henderson J. (2000). *Protecting Indigenous Knowledge and Heritage: A Global Challenge.* Saskatoon: Purich Publishing Ltd.

Bach, M. (2000). "Toward a More Inclusive Definition of Literacy" MTML'S *Incoming* 2 no.3 March 2000 < http://www.mtml.ca/newslet/apr00/page3.htm > (25 May 2004)

Beauchesne, E. (2005). "Poverty in Canada substantially underestimated, reveal statistics". *Can West News Service*, 13 May, <http://ccsd.ca/media/2005/povrecalc.pdf > (13 May 2005)

Beavis, M., Klos N., Carter T. and Douchant C. (1997). *Literature Review Aboriginal People and Homelessness.* University of Winnipeg, <http://www.cmhc-schl.gc.ca/en/imquaf/ho/abpeho001.cfm?renderforprint+1> (25 May 2004).

Beck, P., Walters A. and Francisco N. (1993).*The Sacred: Ways of Knowledge, Sources of Life.* 3rd ed.Tsaile, Arizona: Navajo Community College Press.

Belfore, M. (2002). *Good Practice in Use: Guidelines for Good Practice in Workplace Education.* Toronto: Ontario Literacy Coalition.

Bell, D. (2004). *Sharing Our Success: Ten Case Studies in Aboriginal Schooling*. Kelowna, B.C.: Society for the Advancement of Excellence in Education.

Bird, J., Land L. and Macadam M. (2002). eds. *Nation to Nation: Aboriginal Sovereignty and the Future of Canada*. Toronto: Irwin Publishing.

Brant, J. and George P. (1997). *Native Literacy Planning Process: Survey Results*. Owen Sound: Ontario Native Literacy Coalition.

Bussidor, I. and Bilgen-Reinart, U. (1997). *Night Spirits: The Story of the Relocation of the Sayisi Dene*. Winnipeg: University of Manitoba Press.

Boldt, M. and Long, A. (1985). *The Quest for Justice: Aboriginal Peoples and Aboriginal Rights*. Toronto: University of Toronto Press

Boldt, M. (1993). *Surviving as Indians: the Challenge of Self-Government*. Toronto: University of Toronto Press, 1993.

Bossort, P., Monnastes C., and Malnarich G. (1990). eds. *Conference Report Literacy 2000: Make the Next Ten Years Matter*.

Canadian Council on Social Development. (1998). *Family Violence in a Patriarchal Culture: A Challenge to Our Way of Living*. Ottawa: The Keith Press Ltd.

Canadian Education Association. (2004). *Policy Brief: the Promise and Problem of Literacy for Canada: an Agenda for Action*, <http://www.literacy.ca/public/pbrief/cover.htm> (28 October 2004).

Canadian Education Association. (2003). *Focus on Research and Policy: Literacy as a Public Policy Issue*, <http://www.cea-ace.ca/foo.cfm?subsection=lit&page=pol> (15 February 2005).

Canadian Race Relations Foundation (CRRF). (2002). *Learning About Walking in Beauty: Placing Aboriginal Perspectives in Canadian Classrooms*. Toronto: Canadian Race Relations Foundation

Castellano, M.B., Davis L. and Lahache L. (2000). eds. *Aboriginal Education: Fulfilling the Promise*. Vancouver/Toronto: UBC Press.

Castellano, M. (2000). "Updating Aboriginal Traditions of Knowledge." in *Indigenous Knowledges in Global Contexts*. eds. Dei et al. Toronto: University of Toronto Press

Chapman I., Newhouse D., and McCaskill D. (1991). "Management in Contemporary Aboriginal Organizations". *Canadian Journal of Native Studies* 11 no.2, < http://www.brandon.ca/Library/cjns/11.2/McCaskill.pdf > (9 September 2003)

Chrisjohn, R., Young S. and Maraun M. (1997). *The Circle Game: Shadows and Substance in the Indian Residential School Experience in Canada*. Penticton: Theytus Books Lt

Coalition for the Advancement of Aboriginal Studies. (2002). *Learning about Walking in Beauty: Placing Aboriginal Perspectives in Canadian Classrooms*. Toronto: Canadian Race Relations Foundation.

Cockell, J. and Penney M. (2001). *Adult First Nations Students with Special Needs* submitted to First Nations Education Steering Committee, < www.fnesco.bc.ca > (4 December 2004).

Coulman, J. A. (2003). *Education in Ontario: Education Resources and the Mental Health of Children and Youth*, < http://www.ontario.cmha.ca/ > (4 December 2004).

Crosson-Tower, C. (1999). *Understanding Child Abuse and Neglect*. 4th ed. Toronto: Allyn and Bacon.

Cunliff, A. L. (2003). "Reflexive Inquiry Organizational Research: Questions and Possibilities" *Human Relations* 56(8) 983-1003. London: Sage Publishing.

Dauenhauer, N. and Dauenhauer, R. (1999). "The Paradox of Talking on the Page: some Aspects of the Tlinget and Haida Experience." in Murray and Rice *Talking on The Page: Editing Aboriginal Texts*. Toronto: University of Toronto Press

Darville, R. (1992). "Adult Literacy Work in Canada." *Canadian Association for Adult Education: Centre for Policy Studies in Education – UBC*, <http://www.nald.ca/fulltext> (14 February 2005).

Dei, G., Hall, B., and Rosenberg, D. (2000) eds. *Indigenous Knowledges in Global Contexts: Multiple Readings of Our World*. Toronto: University of Toronto Press

Deloria Jr. V. (1997). *Red Earth White Lies: Native Americans and the Myth of Scientific Fact*. Golden: Fulcrum Publishing.

Densmore, F. (1979). *Chippewa Customs*. St. Paul: Minnesota Historical Society Press.

Christopher Duchesne, "Re: defining isolated," 23 February 2005, personal email (24 February 2005)

Dumont, J. (1993). "Justice and Aboriginal People." *Royal Commission on Aboriginal Peoples, Aboriginal Peoples and the Justice System: Report of the National Round Table on Aboriginal Justice Issues*. Ottawa: Supply and Services.

Dupuis, R. (2002). *Justice for Canada's Aboriginal Peoples*. Translators: Robert Chodos, and Susan Joanis, Toronto: James Lorimer & Company Ltd., Publishers

Etkin, C., (1991). "Native Literacy Programs: Two Case Studies in Implementation" *Canadian Journal of Native Studies* 11 no.2, <www.brandon.ca/Library/CJNS/11.2/etkin.pdf > (9 September 2003)

Fallis, R. (1998). "The Quality of School Matters." *Transition Magazine* 28 no.1, <http://vifamiy.ca/library/transition/281/281.html> (28 October 3004).

Farrell, S.J., Aubrey T. and Reissing E. (2002). *Street Needs Assessment: an Investigation of the Characteristics and Service Needs of Persons Who areHomeless and not Currently Using Emergency Shelters in Ottawa.* Health, Recreation and Social Services Committee of the City of Ottawa,<www.spcottawa.on.ca > (4 December 2004).

Folinsbee, S. (2001). *Briefing Paper: Literacy and the Canadian Workforce*, Prepared for the Movement for Canadian Literacy, <http://www.literacy.ca/public/brief> (18 October 2004).

Friere, P. (1985). *The Politics of Education: Culture, Power, and Liberation.* CT: Bergin & Garvey Publishers, Inc.

Friere, P. and Macedo D. (1987). *Literacy: Reading the Word and the World.* CT: Bergin & Garvey Publishers, Inc.

Friere, P. (2000 a). *Pedagogy of the Oppressed.* 30th Anniversary Edition. NY: Continuum

Friere, P. (2000 b). *Education for Critical Consciousness.* NY: Continuum

Gaikezheyongai, S. (2000). *Aboriginal Enhanced Access to Native Learning: A Literacy Project.* Toronto: Native Women's Resource Center.

George, P. (1993). *Empowering People and Building Competent Communities*. Prepared for Literacy Branch Ontario Ministry of Education and Training.

George, P. (1998). *Position Paper on Program Reform*. Owen Sound: Ontario Native Literacy Coalition.

Gibbs, M. (1988). *The Necessity of a Unique Definition of Native Psychology of Behavior and Personality*. Unpublished Paper. Gabriel Dumont Institute.

Gillani, B.B. (1994). *Application of Vygotsky's Social Cognitive Theory to the Design of Instructional Materials*: unpublished doctoral dissertation, University of Southern California, <http://elleads.csuhayward.edu/chapter1NewChallenges.pdf> (17 September 2003).

Government of Canada. (1996). *Reading the Future: a Portrait of Literacy in Canada:Backgrounder on the International Adult Literacy Survey*, <http://www.statcan.ca/english/freepub/89F0094XIE/backge.pdf> (2 January 2003).

Government of Canada. (2003). *Response to Raising Adult Literacy Skills: The Need for a Pan-Canadian Response*. Ottawa: Queens Printers.

Grant, A. (1996). *No End to Grief: Indian Residential Schools in Canada*. Winnipeg: Pemmican Publications Inc.

Graveline, J. F. (1998). *Circle Works: Transforming Eurocentric Consciousness*. Halifax: Fernwood Publishing.

Grieve, K. (2003). *Supporting Learning, Supporting Change: A Research Project on Self-Management & Self-direction*. Toronto: Ontario Literacy.

Grieve, K. (2004). *Supporting Learning, Supporting Change: Developing an Approach to Helping Learners Build Self-awareness and Self-direction.* Toronto: Ontario Literacy.

Gunn Allen, P. (1992). *The Sacred Hoop: Recovering the Feminine in American Indian Traditions.* Boston: Beacon Press.

Haddad, T. and Spivey M. (1992). "All or Nothing: Modernization, Dependency and Wage Labour on a Reserve in Canada". *Canadian Journal of Native Studies* 12 no.2, www.brandon.ca/library/CJNS/12.2/default.htm (9 September 2003)

Hiag-Brown, C. (1998). "Taking Control: Contradiction and First Nations Adult Education." in Battiste and Barman *First Nations Education in Canada the Circle Un*folds

Hamilton, Mary. 2001. "Privileged Literacies: Policy, Institutional Process and the Life of the IALS". *Language and Education*, 15 (2001), 2 & 3 pp 178-196
< www.literaciesjournal.ca/articles/fall03/webartic/exerpt3.htm >
(8 November 2003)

Hampton, E. (1995). "Redefinition of Education" in Battiste and Barman, *First Nations Education in Canada: the Circle unfolds.* Vancouver: UBC Press.

Haley, D. and Davidson J. (2000). *A Brutal Way of Learning: Does It Have To Be?* Peterborough: Davidson Communications.

Hart, M.A. (2002). *Seeking Mino-Pimatisiwn: An Aboriginal Approach to Helping.* Halifax: Fernwood Publishing.

Hargrave, C. (2004). *Homelessness in Canada: from Housing to Shelters to Blankets,* <http://www.shareintl.org/archives/homelessness/hl-ch Canada.htm> (17 October 2004).

Harwood, C. (2001). *Handbook for Literacy Tutors.* NC: Grassroots Press.

Henson, J.E. (1982). "Pedagogy and Politics in Native Literacy projects: the Case of the Native Adult Learning Group." The Canadian Journal of Native Studies 2 no.1 (1982), < www.brandonu. ca/Library/CJNS/2.1/henson.pdf > (9 September 2003)

Hill, B.H. (2002). *Shaking the Rattle: Healing the Trauma of Colonization.* Six Nations of the Grand River: Shadyhat Books.

Hill, D.L. (1995). *Aboriginal Access to Post-Secondary Education: Prior Learning Assessment and its Use within Aboriginal Programs of Learning.* Ontario: F.N.T.I. Loyalist College.

Hill, D. L. (1999). *Holistic Learning: A Model of Education Based on Aboriginal Cultural Philosophy.* Unpublished thesis. Saint Francis Xavier University.

Hill, K. (2001). *Culture Based Curriculum: A Framework.* Owen Sound: Ontario Native Literacy Coalition.

Horsman, J. (1999). *Too Scared to Learn: Women, Violence and Education.* Toronto: McGilligan Books.

Horsman, J. (1998). *But I'm Not a Therapist: Furthering Discussion about Literacy Work with Survivors of Trauma,* <http://www.jennyhorsman. com> (24 January 2005)

Horsman, J. (2004). The *Challenge to Create a Safer Learning Environment for Youth,* <http://www.jennyhorsman.com/ challengetocreate_FinalCopy.pdf> (13 February 2005)

Human Resources Development Canada (HRDC). (2000). "Adult Literacy: Policies, Programs and Practices Lessons Learned". *Final Report Evaluation and Data Development*, < http://www11.hrdc-drhc.gc.ca > (17 February 2005)

Human Resources and Skills Development Canada. (2005). *Call for proposals: Research Partners Projects*, <http://hrsdc.gc./ca/en/hip/11d/nls/callrpeopen.shtml> (25 February 2005).

Hylton, J. (1999). *Aboriginal Self-Government in Canada: Current Trends and Issues*. Saskatoon: Purich Publishing Ltd.

Indian and Northern Affairs. (2003). fall 2002. Survey of First Nations People Living on-Reserve-Final Report HTML, < http://www.aiiinc-inac.gc.ca/nr/prs/j-a2003/2-02240_e.html > (8 March 2003)

Indian and Northern Affairs. (2004). *Band Classification Manual*, < http://www.ainc-inac.gc.ca/pub/fnnrg/bcm e.html > (23 February 2005)

Irwin, L. (2000). ed. *Native American Spirituality: A Critical Reader*. Lincoln: University of Nebraska Press.

Jackson T., McCaskill D. and Hall B.L. (1982). eds. "Learning for Self-Determination: Community Based Options for Native Training and Research". *Canadian Journal of Native Studies* 2 no.1, < www.brandon.ca/Library/CJNS/2.1/introd.pdf > (9 September 2003)

Jones C. (2003). "Self-Management and Self-Direction in the Success of Native Literacy Learners. Advancing Aboriginal Languages and Literacy." *The Canadian Journal of Native Education 27* no.1 (2003)

Jones, K. (1 August 2000). Canada State Witch Hunt of Advocates for Toronto's Homeless, http://www.wsws.org/articles/2000/aug2000/toro-a02_prn.shtml> (25 May 2004).

Kendall, F. E. *Understanding White Privilege*, 2001: 1-10,<http:// www.alumni.berkley.edu/Students/Leadership/Online> (11 March 2004).

Kirkness, V. and Bowman S. (1992). First Nations and Schools: Triumphs and Struggles. Toronto: Canadian Educational Association in CRRF 2002: 163

Knockwood, I. (1992). *Out of the Depths: The Experiences of Mi'kmaw Children at the Indian Residential School at Shubenacadie, Nova Scotia.* Lockeport: Roseway Publishing.

Kuhn, P. and Sweetman A. (2002). *Aboriginals as Unwilling Immigrants: Contact, Assimilation and Labour Market Outcomes.* <http://www.turtleisland.org> (23 November 2004).

Lamontagne, F. (2004). "The Aboriginal Work Force: What Lies Ahead CLBC Commentary". *Canadian Labour and Business Centre.* < www.clbc.ca/files/reports/Aboriginal_Commentary_Piece.pdf > (14 November 2004)

Lane, P., Bopp M., Bopp J. and Brown L. (2003). *The Sacred Tree.* 3rd ed. Lethbridge: Four Worlds International Institute._

Lepine, R. (2003). *Strengthening Community Partnerships.* Owen Sound: Ontario Native Literacy Coalition.

Literacy Alberta. *Fact Sheets #7 Literacy and Aboriginal Success, Fact Sheet #9 Literacy and Poverty, Fact Sheet #12 Literacy and Learning Disabilities* <http://www.literacy-alberta.ca/facts.htm> (15 October 2004).

Logan-Elliott, A. and McClain K. (2003). *Phase II Field Development: Moving Towards Action.* Owen Sound: Ontario Native Literacy Coalition.

Long, D. and Dickason O., (2000). eds. *Visions of the Heart: Canadian Aboriginal Issues.*2nd ed. Toronto: Harcourt Canada.

Longfield, J. (2003). *Raising Adult Literacy Skills: The Need for a Pan-Canadian Response.* Ottawa: Communication Canada.

Maracle, Lee. (1996). *I Am Woman: A Native Perspective on Sociology and Feminism.* Vancouver: Press Gang Publishers

Marshall, G. (1998). *Oxford Dictionary of Sociology.* New York: Oxford University Press.

McNab, D. (1999). *Circles of Time: Aboriginal Land Rights and Resistance in Ontario.* Waterloo: Wilfred Laurier Press.

Mercredi, O. and Turpel, M. E. (1993). *In the Rapids: Navigating the Future of First Nations.* Toronto: Penguin Books.

Middelton- Moz, J. (1989). *Children of Trauma: Rediscovering Your Discarded Self.* Washington: Health Communications Inc.

Mikulecky, L. (1990) "Literacy for What Purpose?" in Venezky, Wagner, Ciliberte *Toward Defining Literacy.* Newark DE: International Reading Association.

Miller, J.R. (2004). *Lethal Legacy: Current Native Controversies in Canada.* Toronto: McClelland & Stewart Ltd.

Milloy, J. A. (1999). *National Crime: The Canadian Government and the Residential School System 1879 to 1986.* Winnipeg: University of Manitoba Press.

Ministry of Community and Social Services. 1997. Ontario Works Act. 1997. Ontario Regulation 134/98 Amended to O. Reg. 417/04, < http://192.75.156.68/DBLaws/Regs/English/980134_e.htm > (15 February 2005)

Ministry of Education. 2001. Ontario Curriculum Planner: Kindergarten – Grade 12

Ministry of Education/ Ministry of Training, Colleges and Universities (2001). *Backgrounder: Ontario Support of Literacy Projects Strengthens Employment and Learning Skills*, <http://edu.gov.on.ca/eng/document/nr/01.11/bg1102.html > (17 March 2005)

Ministry of Education and Training: Literacy Branch. (1993). *Empowering the Spirit of Native People: The Native Literacy Movement in* Ontario. Ontario: Queen's Printer.

Ministry of Education: Ministry of Training, Colleges and Universities. (2002) *Literacy in Ontario: the Rewards are for Life*, <http://www.edu.gov.on.ca> (21 August 2002).

Ministry of Education: Ministry of Training, Colleges and Universities. 2004. *Policy/Program Memorandum No. 127: The Secondary School Literacy Graduation Requirement*, <http://www.edu.gov.on.ca/extra/eng/ppm/127.html> (17 October 2004).

Minister of Supply and Services Canada. (1996). *People to People, Nation to Nation: Highlights from the Report of the Royal Commission on Aboriginal Peoples (RCAP)*. Ottawa: Supply and Services Canada.

Ministry of Training, Colleges and Universities. (2000). *Literacy and Basic Skills (LBS) Program Guidelines*. Workforce Preparation Branch. Ontario: Queen's Printer.

Ministry of Training, Colleges and Universities. (2005). *Literacy and Basic Skills Program Monitoring Report, 2004-2005.*

Monture-Angus, P. (1995). *Thunder in My Soul: A Mohawk Woman Speaks.* Halifax: Fernwood Publishing.

Monture-Angus, P. (1999). *Journeying Forward: Dreaming First Nations Independence*. Halifax: Fernwood Publishing.

Movement for Canadian Literacy Submission to the House of Commons Standing Committee on Finance. (2002). *Literacy Matters: Why Canada Should Make Adult Literacy and Essential Skills a Policy and Funding Priority* 2002, <http://www.literacy.ca/govrel/matters/cover.htm> (15 October 2004).

Mullaly, B. (1997). *Structural Social Work*. 2nd ed. Don Mills: Oxford University Press.

Munby, H. and Russell T. (1994). "The Authority of Experience in Learning How to Teach: Messages from a Physics Methods Class," *Journal of Teacher Education* 45, no.2, March/April 1994, <http://educ.queensu.ca/~russellt/howteach/1994a.htm> (19 November 2004).

Murray, L. J. and Rice K. (1999). eds. *Talking on the Page: Editing Aboriginal Oral Texts*. Toronto: University of Toronto Press.

National Anti-Poverty Organization. (1992). *Literacy and Poverty: A View from the Inside*. Summary Report. Ottawa: Movement for Canadian Literacy, <http://www.literacy.ca/litand/9.htm > (15 October 2004).

Native Literacy Research Report. (1993). *You Took my Talk*. Report for the Standing Committee on Aboriginal Affairs, House of Commons Canada. B.C. Okanagan College: Native Adult Education Centre.

Newman, M. (1994). *Defining the Enemy: Adult Education in Social Action*. Sydney: Stewart Victor Publishing.

Ontario Literacy Coalition. *First Sites Report: Collective Consultation on Workforce/Workplace Literacy*, 2003, <http://www.alphaplus.ca/opnhs/english/Sitelist> (17 October 2004).

Ontario Training and Adjustment Board. (1994). *Framework and Quality Standards for Adult Literacy Education in Ontario.* Toronto: OTAB

Phonovisual. Products, Inc. (1978). *The Phonovisual Method,* <http://www.phonovisual.com> (10 June 2005)

Ponting, R. J., (1986). ed. *Arduous Journey: Canadian Indians and Colonization.* Toronto: McClelland and Stewart Limited.

Resolution of the 5th Annual Elder's Conference. (1980). *Plastic Medicine Men.* < http://users.pandora.be/gohiyuhi/articles/art00039.htm > (10 July 2005)

Reyhner, J., Martin J., Lockard L., and Sakiestewa G. W. (2000). eds. *Learn in Beauty: Indigenous Education for a New Century.* Flagstaff Arizona: Northern Arizona University.

Ristock, J. L. and Pennell J. (1996). *Community Research as Empowerment: Feminist Links, Postmodern Interruptions.* Toronto: Oxford University Press.

Roeher Institute. (1999). *Literacy, Disability and Communication: Making the Connection.* Toronto: York University

Rodriguez, C. and Sawyer D. (1990). *Native Literacy Research Report.* British Columbia: Ministry of Advanced Education, Training and Technology.

Rosenthal, R. and Jacobson, L. (1992) *Pygmalion in the Classroom: Teacher Expectations and Pupil's Intellectual Development.* New York: Irvington Publishers.

Ross, R. (1996). *Returning to the Teachings: Exploring Aboriginal Justice.* Toronto: Penguin Books.

Royal Commission on Aboriginal Peoples (RCAP). (1993). *The Path to Healing: Report of the National Roundtable*, < http://www.ubcic. bc.ca/docs/Path to Healing.doc >(4 February 2003).

Saskatchewan Indian Institute of Technologies. (1990). *Aboriginal Literacy Action Plan: a Literacy Practitioners' Guide to Action*. Saskatoon: Saskatchewan Indian Institute of Technologies.

Scaldwell, W. A. (1989). "Effect of Otitis Media upon Reading Scores of Indian Children in Ontario". *Journal of American Indian Education* 28 no.2 <http://jaie.asu.edu/v28/V27S2eff.htm> (1 August 2003)

Shore, S. (2003). "What's Whiteness got to do with it?" *Literacies: Researching Practice, Practicing Research* 2 (fall 2003):19-25.

Smith, L. Tuhiwai. (1999). *Decolonizing Methodologies: Research and Indigenous People*. New York: Zed Books Ltd.

Social Sciences, University of Ottawa. (2004). *Presentation to the National Secretariat on Homelessness and Death: A Social Autopsy Study*. Ottawa: University of Ottawa Social Sciences Department, <http://www.socialsciences.uottawa.ca/cvcs/eng/publ.asp> (18 October 2004).

Spielmann, R. (1998). *You're so fat! Exploring Ojibwe Discourse*. Toronto: University of Toronto Press Incorporated.

Statistics Canada. (2001). *Selected Labour Force Characteristics (50), Registered Indian Status (3), Age Groups (5A), for Population 15 Years and Over, for Canada, Provinces, Territories and Census Metropolitan Areas*, <http://www.ca:8096/bsolc/english/ bsolc?catno=97F0011XIE2001052 > (18 October 2004)

Sussman S. (2003). *Moving the Markers: New Perspectives on Adult Literacy Rates in Canada*. Ottawa: Movement for Canadian Literacy.

Tinker, G. (1993). *Missionary Conquest: the Gospel and Native American Cultural Genocide*. Minneapolis: Fortress Press

Thompson, K. (2002). *Practitioner Standards Model Development Project*. Owen Sound: Ontario Native Literacy Coalition.

Toronto Correspondent. The Social Significance of Toronto's June 15 Homeless "Riot", 24 June 2000, <http://www.wsws.org/articles/2000/jun2000/tor-j24_prn.shtml> (May 2004)

United Nations Educational Scientific and Cultural Organization (UNESCO). (2003) *United Nations Literacy Decade*, < http://portal.unesco.org/education/ev.php > (2 December 2003)

Veeman, N. (2002). *Improving Adult Literacy Levels: a Critical Look at GovernmentStrategies and Public Awareness Campaigns*, <http://www.usask.ca/education/alcs/papers/veemanl.pdf> (16 September 2002).

Venezky, R. L., Wagner D.A., and Ciliberte B.S. (1990). eds. *Toward Defining Literacy*. Newark DE: International Reading Association.

Venezky, R. L. (1992). *Matching Literacy Testing with Social Policy: What are the Alternatives?*, <http://www.nald.ca/fulltext/report4/rep36-40/rep39-01.htm> (2 January 2003).

Weinstein, L., and Lewis D. (1998). "Making Connections: Approaches to Adult Literacy". *Transition Magazine* 29 no.1, <http://www.vifamily.ca/library/transition/281/281.html> (28 October 2004).

Williams, L. and Wyatt, J. (1994). "Training Indian Teachers in a Community Setting: The Mount Currie Lil'wat Programme" in Barman et al 1994.

Wooden Indians & Stereotypical Imagery
<<u>http://www.iaiancad.org/nep/courses/indig1/humor/chapters/</u>
<u>woodenindians.html #powerful</u> > (9 July 2005)

www.ingramcontent.com/pod-product-compliance
Lightning Source LLC
Chambersburg PA
CBHW051439280526
45785CB00003B/1345